Love and Pornography

Love and Pornography

Dealing with Porn and
Saving Your Relationship

Victoria Prater and Garry Prater

True Wind
PUBLISHING

Published 2009

Library of Congress Control Number: 2009900487
Classifications:
1. Sex addiction
2. Sex addicts — rehabilitation
3. Internet pornography — United States
4. Sex in mass media — United States
5. Sex addiction — treatment
6. Pornography — Social aspects

ISBN 978-0-9818743-8-8

BISAC Classifications:
HEA042000   Sexuality
FAM027000   Interpersonal Relations

The paper used in this publication is acid free and lignin free.
It meets all ANSI standards for archival quality paper.

Printed in the United States of America.

Grateful acknowledgement is made for permission to reprint the previously published material:
"The Guest House" "Out beyond ideas" by Jelaluddin Rumi, translated by Coleman Barks, published in *Selected Poems of Rumi* (New York: Penguin, 1995). Reprinted by permission of Coleman Barks.

True Wind Publishing

www.GetHelpwithPorn.com

.

For Robert Gonzales, who made this book possible
with his patient and persistent invitations
to see the essential life in everything.

The Guest House

This being human is a guest house.
Every morning a new arrival.

A joy, a depression, a meanness,
some momentary awareness comes
as an unexpected visitor.

Welcome and entertain them all!
Even if they're a crowd of sorrows,
who violently sweep your house
empty of its furniture,
still, treat each guest honorably.
He may be clearing you out
for some new delight.

The dark thought, the shame, the malice,
meet them at the door laughing,
and invite them in.

Be grateful for whoever comes,
because each has been sent
as a guide from beyond.

—Rumi, translated by Coleman Barks

Contents

Acknowledgments

uthor may be defined as one who creates, causes, or originates. Thus, the true author of this book is the life-changing experience we have shared. Much as the seed is credited with creating a tree, our names get the credit on the cover, but this book would never have existed without the nurturing support of many others. We would like to express our immense gratitude to the co-creators of the book.

Many, many thanks go to Marshall Rosenberg for creating a body of knowledge that is reverberating around the world in so many wonderful ways. This book is our expression of the gift you have given us by presenting Nonviolent Communication to the world.

Thank God Teresa Cutler-Boyles of Inkwell, Inc. came on board early. It seemed that something cosmic was at play when we connected. She believed in us and this project right from the start and never wavered in her support. (Did your mom tie your mittens on a string and pull them through your coat so you could relax and not worry that you were going to lose them? That's what it's like working with Teresa.) Her ability to hold a project of this magnitude and her skill with the written word had us thinking we could let go and trust that it would happen. Thank you, Teresa, for seeing the promise in this book and for your constant encouragement that we could do this!

Next on board were Sheridan McCarthy and Stanton Nelson from Meadowlark Publishing Services. As soon as we connected by phone with Sheridan, we knew we were in the presence of a guardian angel sent from the heavens. Writing a book seemed a lot like having a baby. We were protective of it and nurtured it every day, and couldn't bear the thought of letting just anybody take care of it. Sheridan and Stan are the ultimate book nannies. With their skills and knowledge of the book world we could hand our baby to them, knowing without a shadow of a doubt that it would be well taken care of every step of the way. Thank you, Sheridan and Stan!

Thanks, Dr. Bruce Derman, for your support during difficult times and for your book *We'd Have a Great Relationship if It Weren't for You*. And thanks for your help in getting started writing and making connections in the writing world.

Thanks so much to all of you who took the time to fill out our survey on porn! Many people did, and many of those anonymously, and we hope you know we appreciate the time you took to do it.

More waves of appreciation to all those who read a chapter here and there and provided feedback and editing: Evelyn Schouela, Rachael McDavid, Raphaella Lewis, Ann McNight, Michele Lavery, Julia Sauder, John DeFoe, Jay Glick, Gregg Kendrick, and Mary Zukowski. We are hoping that is everyone, but alas, it has been a long journey and there have been many contributors along the way, so if we missed you, please know that we are grateful.

Victoria would like to personally thank the many people in the Nonviolent Communication community who worked closely with her as well as other friends and family members who contributed to this book.

Much gratitude goes to Bob Metz, whom I treasure as my friend and mentor. I appreciate that he models NVC for me in the way he lives his life. Thanks, Bob, for taking me into your life so fully and quickly—I treasure all of our wonderful conversations and your patience and persistence in getting this transformative work across to me. Your contributions and editing were invaluable.

Thanks to Sylvia Haskvitz, who brought both NVC and editing skills to the book. Thank you for awakening my inner Sherlock Holmes and teaching me to be a great needs sleuth!

I am so grateful to my NVC Life Group, which has been a container for learning and love since our beginning. Thanks for holding steady through all my porn conversations!

Kelly Bryson loved the idea of this book from the beginning and didn't criticize my writing, even in its beginning stages when I imagine it was tough to read. You were such a wonderful source of support for me while I was in California. Thanks for all our thought-provoking conversations.

Waves of appreciation go to Wes Taylor and Mark Schultz for all the wonderful conversations and perspectives you have shared with me. Some of the things we talked about are surely embedded in this book. Also, Mark, thanks for your continued support in the technical world of the Internet.

Thanks to Ann Furniss, who has a greater gift for words than anyone I know. I appreciate that you not only helped some in editing but took the time to coach me on how to write dialogue. I still think the world needs more of your writing!

Thanks to both my sisters for always—and I do mean always—believing in me.

To my long time friends Zantui Rose and Paul Seidman: I still think of us as the three musketeers committed to transforming the doughnut. This book has seeds that go back to our college days. As always, your presence in my life has contributed to my being a person who is increasingly in alignment with my own integrity, and it has supported this book in reflecting that. Thank you both for your love and support and your fierce lifelong commitments to truth and justice.

And last but *certainly* not least, a deep bow of gratitude goes to Linnaea Marvell, whose contribution in shaping the end product was so valuable. By some standards I was finished with the book much earlier, but I had a nagging and persistent feeling of anxiety that it still wasn't right. I asked Linnaea if she would have a look at a chapter, and within a few minutes she named what it was that needed to change. Waves of relief washed over me when she came on board, and I knew that she was someone who had the vision that would carry this book to completion. Thank you, sister and soul mate, for your x-ray vision to penetrate the surface levels and get down to the essence of life.

These acknowledgements are not complete without addressing how much the two of us owe one another. This book is more than the story of how we saved our relationship; it's the story of how we grew into our true selves. It would never have happened without Victoria's courage and determination and Garry's dogged desire to be honest and open. In working together to create this book, we have fortified our connection to each other and built the foundation for a wonderful relationship. Together, we created this book out of our love for each other and our wish to share it with the world.

Preface

This is the book we wish had existed when we began navigating the difficult issue of pornography three years ago. When we searched for help, the resources we found either focused on suppressing the symptoms of porn addiction or argued that it was right or wrong. We didn't want to embrace yet another message that there was something *wrong* with us, and we didn't want to have to hide parts of ourselves for the sake of the relationship. Instead, we wanted a way to deal with this challenge that gave us a greater understanding and acceptance of ourselves and each other.

Our struggles took us to the bedrock of our characters and to the verge of breaking up several times. But clinging to the connection between us, and with the help of some wonderful mentors and guides, we found a way to heal ourselves and save our relationship. As we began to change and grow, and as our relationship became a source of strength rather than pain and tension, we felt a rising sense of confidence and freedom that we wanted to share with others.

Toni Morrison once said, "If there's a book you really want to read but it hasn't been written yet, then you must write it." This was not easy advice to follow given the subject matter we were dealing with. With great trepidation about exposing our fears and vulnerabilities, we began the work. To our surprise and relief, we found that our first tentative explorations and ideas were met with enthusiasm and support, and that gave us the courage to keep going. Once started, it seemed that the book had a destiny of its own and we just happened to be along for the ride.

This isn't a book of definitive answers or quick fixes. It isn't about figuring out who is right and who is wrong. It's about looking beyond our own and another's actions to see what really motivates us. Once we can clearly see what we actually need instead of focusing our attention on the action, a whole new world of possible choices opens to us.

There is a place we all share as human beings; Rumi, the great Sufi poet and mystic, described it as a field "out beyond ideas of rightdoing and wrongdoing." This is the place where true understanding and healing can occur. We believe he is referring to our essence, and when we see this essence of ourselves and others, our connection to all of life is restored. This is the source of true strength and compassion. We have discovered that Rumi's field isn't a place only some of us have or only some of us can see—it is in everyone, and it is accessible to all.

What you will find in these pages will help you to understand and accept yourself and others in any situation. Here we introduce you to principles that will help you navigate any issue in your life and build stronger relationships. If your partner looks at porn and you're worried that he or she won't want to read this with you, rest assured; simply shifting your own relationship to the issue can create amazing results in your relationship. And if you are the one looking at porn, this book will give you a better understanding of why you might be so attracted to it. It will give you more choices and the ability to step back and assess the attraction.

We invite you to join us in this field out beyond rightdoing and wrongdoing. It is our hope that this book will help you gain greater self-awareness, restore your relationship, and find true intimacy and love.

chapter 1:
The Journey Begins

Victoria, I have something I want to tell you," my fiancé began. "I don't want any surprises or secrets between us. And I don't want to hide this, or feel shame about it like I have in the past." He paused and took a breath, then plunged ahead. "The thing is, I like to look at porn."

This simple declaration took our relationship on an unexpected detour, well off the beaten path.

Several years ago I began seeing Garry again, a man with whom I'd had a relationship eighteen years earlier. Much can happen to people in eighteen years, and this was certainly true of us. At the time we reconnected, Garry had left a marriage three years earlier and I had just ended a three-year relationship. In some ways, it was as if we had never parted, but the growth we had both experienced in the intervening years had given us a capacity for much deeper intimacy than we'd had before. Along with the joy and ease we always felt together, we seemed better equipped for the art of loving. Quickly, we knew we wanted to be together, and we became engaged.

One of Garry's patterns in earlier relationships had been to hide what he believed were unacceptable parts of himself, which had the unintended effect of virtually ensuring that he would not experience the intimacy he longed for. He was determined to change this pattern, and he chose to be open with me about who he was. When he told me about his longtime pattern of viewing pornography, I felt no small measure of discomfort, but I found that his honesty and openness, and his willingness to be who he was and to share that person with me, deepened my love and respect for him. For the time being, I accepted the situation, and we began working on the issue and my unease with it.

We were still working on it when an unexpected job opportunity for Garry compelled us to decide about living together much sooner than we had expected: his new position meant moving across the country. Garry had often moved for his job and had no strong attachments to where he was living, but such a move would take me far from my work, friends, and community on the East Coast. After weeks of deliberation, we decided that the gains outweighed the risks, and so we moved to California together.

My personal "crash" came soon after we arrived and settled into a rented house. Suddenly I found myself with no systems of support—and only when they were gone did I realize how much I had relied on them. Without my work, I felt lost, lacking purpose. I was meeting new people but didn't yet have friends, and the time difference and our conflicting schedules made it difficult for me to reach out to my friends back east. Exploring my new home helped pass some time. The seaside town where we lived was as spectacularly beautiful as calendar art, but for me it was every bit as flat; I felt no connection at all to the place. With no real friends and nothing to do that had any meaning, my feelings of isolation grew. I was profoundly lonely, and I felt as if my very identity was dissolving. I had pulled the plug on my former life, and the only connection I had left was with Garry. I began to focus more and more of my energy on him, both positive and negative. And one of the things I fixated on was his desire for porn.

We were sharing a computer now, and the amount of porn he was viewing was literally in my face. Each time I entered a web address or search term, the computer offered a list of possibilities I might be looking for based on previous sites visited. My stomach pitched when I saw the choices. While the list of porn sites seemed quite long—an issue in itself—what bothered me most was that I couldn't get away from it. No matter what I entered, porn sites were always an option.

I was suddenly terrified. This habit was no longer okay ... *he* was no longer okay. I asked myself, "Who is this person I'm with? What does it mean that he needs this kind of stimulation in his life? Is there something wrong with the relationship? Is there something wrong with *me?*"

GARRY: *I knew that this move was a big change for Victoria, especially since she'd left so much behind, and now that I could see she was starting to have some doubts about the move, I felt guilty. I tried to reassure her that looking at porn had nothing to do with how I felt about her, but I could tell that she didn't believe me. I also couldn't explain my desire to look at porn, and it wasn't something I was ready to give up. In a way, it was like an old friend.*

I found myself becoming more and more secretive. I felt shame and started to hide what I was doing from her so she wouldn't be upset. If she walked in while I was looking at it, I quickly clicked off and pretended that I was looking at something else. This only exacerbated Victoria's fears because she could sense the dishonesty. We were beginning a vicious cycle fueled by guilt, shame, fear, and distrust.

I had a sense of dread. I started to wonder if I'd done the right thing by telling her the truth. Some things are best left unsaid; maybe this was one of them.

There was no doubt: I was worried. Garry liked his porn. He would come home from work and sit down at the computer and unwind by surfing the web for pictures of women that stimulated him. While he perused a variety of types, his favorites to look at were young, beautiful nude women, and he liked reading erotic stories.

I hated it that he looked at other women's bodies for hours on end, day after day. I wanted him to take that kind of interest in *my* body and *our* lives together. It brought up many of my insecurities about what I should look like and whether he would judge me in comparison to all those other women. I also worried that he was using porn as a way to numb out and that he wouldn't be able to face the challenges of a real relationship.

GARRY: *I really didn't understand why it was such a big deal that I liked to look at porn. So what? I had hoped that Victoria would be into looking at it with*

*me so we could use it together as a way to have fun.
I also thought that if she didn't have such low self-
esteem, it wouldn't have bothered her as much as it
did. I thought this was her issue, not mine.*

I was livid when he told me that porn was my issue! It
was as if he expected me to say, "Yes, you're right. I'll
just go over here and deal with it all by myself so that
you can keep doing what you want!" Ugh!!

We were deep in conflict and butting heads. I found
myself famished for anything that might ease my pain,
and at the same time, I wanted to understand Garry better. While I still felt too much fear and shame to reach
out to friends, the internet seemed like a safe place to
get some help. Ignoring the porn pop-ups, I sought out
advice columns and articles related to the subject. Much
to my surprise, I found nothing helpful at all. Nothing?
How could this be? Surely there must be people who
had been down this road before me and could share
what worked for them. But instead of what I needed, I
found back-and-forth arguments about porn. These left
me just as unsettled—and worse. I began to feel hopeless.

Most of the arguments fell into one of two camps,
with the language of each side inevitably couched in
terms of good versus evil, right versus wrong. One side
argued that porn freed them from unhealthy inhibitions
and repressions. They stressed the importance of being
allowed the freedom to do as they pleased without fear
of society's reaction. The other side stressed that these
so-called freedoms impinged on the rights of others.
They condemned the users and purveyors of porn for
contributing to the suffering of women and children.

"Porn is a deal breaker. Never tolerate it in a relationship!"

"Looking at porn has nothing to do with the person's partner."

"It's all about the right of freedom."

"Pornography is degrading and offensive to women."

"Looking at porn is contributing to the suffering of those who have been violated."

While I found much of the discussion compelling, and I thought that much of it held some form of truth, none of it was helping me to navigate the angst and confusion in my relationship. I wasn't getting any sense of relief from my distress, nor was I gaining any insight that would help me better understand either Garry's actions or my reactions. I felt righteous one moment and utterly confused the next as I bounced back and forth between the differing poles of right and wrong. I was longing for something that I didn't know how to articulate: something outside the paradigm of polar opposites, something that had room for my pain as well as an understanding of the motives underlying Garry's behavior.

Shadow Territory

Sometimes, after touchdown from my latest trip on the World Wide Web, I wondered what was going on in our culture. If what I was reading was any indication, pornography was a bigger issue than I had ever imagined, with people on all sides suffering in some way because of it. Porn was everywhere, it seemed, so why did I feel so alone with it? How could something be so prevalent yet still so much in the recesses of our culture? Why hadn't I been aware of this before? What was it about porn that kept it hidden, especially in a culture where sexual images abound?

Sex is ever-present in magazines, on television and the internet, in films and on billboards. Some parents dress their little girls in miniature versions of sexy adult clothing and march them across stages to be looked at by adult men and women and then judged on their attractiveness (a theme a suburban family struggled with in the movie *Little Miss Sunshine)*. We see TV commercials with young, sexy girls suggesting that driving this car, dressing in that suit, owning the right stereo means you get the girls (i.e., sex) by extension. And we see young men in Calvin Klein underwear on sidewalk ads in major cities, suggesting that anyone can have the man with the underwear for the right currency: sex.

In these and other ways, sex and images of sex are around us all the time. Our culture is suffused with them; the sexual tension is palpable. One would think we'd be talking about all aspects of it, including porn, but we don't. Many of us have a hard time talking about sex at all, let alone what I call the more *taboo* aspects of it. Oh, we can joke about it, sure, but open, frank dialogue? Forget it.

I wondered if porn was a direct extension of such avoidance. Is it possible that in our reluctance to discuss sex, to confront it directly, we have created a situation in which it has to go *underground* in a sense, to a place where people—like Garry and millions of others—can be free to express themselves without censure? Is it there, in that underground space, where it not only grows but flourishes and becomes magnified?

I recalled the famous psychologist Carl Jung's concept of the shadow, that unconscious part of ourselves that we repress or suppress. Jung believed that the shadow represents everything the conscious person has disowned and rejected in him- or herself, and he emphasized that unless we bring those aspects of the self into conscious awareness, we will be condemned to project those attributes, that essence, onto others. More pertinent to the subject of pornography, that essence would find a way to express itself, often in unrecognizable and distorted ways.

As I contemplated Jung and the debate on the internet, I wondered ... could it be that pornography is one of our culture's expressions of all that we don't dare discuss—its shadow? Is it the collective cultural unconscious resisting the restraints placed on it by our refusal to discuss our sexuality? Or are we longing for something hidden in ourselves, unconsciously trying to find it in pornography? This possibility made sense, and I began to feel hopeful at last. I certainly didn't have all the answers yet, but I finally had a place to start looking.

PARADIGM SHIFT

Concurrent with my contemplation of the shadow, I was looking for something else: a way to understand myself and my reactions, as well as Garry and his desire for pornography, that went beyond all the arguments about right and wrong, moral and immoral. I found a poem by the Sufi poet Rumi that resonated with this desire:

> *Out beyond ideas of wrongdoing and rightdoing*
> *There is a field.*
> *I'll meet you there.*
> *When the soul lies down in that grass,*
> *the world is too full to talk about.*
> *Ideas, language, even the phrase "each other"*
> *doesn't make any sense.*

I realized that I wanted to know this field: in truth, to live in it. I wondered if Garry and I could meet one another out beyond wrongdoing and rightdoing and embrace our distress over porn. For quite a while I held my longing and questions in my heart, not speaking of them even to Garry—until one day the answer came knocking at my door.

I had done some work in the past with Nonviolent Communication (NVC), which has also come to be known as compassionate communication. This is a process developed by Marshall Rosenberg* that is designed to bring forth our natural way of giving and receiving by speaking our truth with honesty and listening with empathy. It supports a quality of connection in which what is deeply valued by each person is equally valued by the other. This is accomplished by connecting to the core values of oneself and others and by clearly express-

*Dr. Marshall B. Rosenberg is the creator of Nonviolent Communication (NVC) and director of educational services for the Center for Nonviolent Communication, an international nonprofit organization. Dr. Rosenberg is author of a number of books we have found useful, including *Nonviolent Communication: A Language of Compassion*.

ing observations, feelings, needs (deeply held values), and requests—while avoiding language that implies that others are wrong.

A few months after arriving in California, and not long after I'd had my realization about the pervasiveness of porn, I invited a local NVC teacher to my home to tell me what training was available locally. As I've experienced with most people I meet in the NVC world, I felt safe and comfortable talking with him about what was going on in my life. When I brought up my angst about Garry's porn, he listened empathetically, which helped settle my anxieties some.

Then I asked, "Why do so many people, including Garry, look at porn?"

"Well," he replied, "looking at porn is just a strategy for meeting needs, so if you can identify the needs he is meeting with it, you will have your answer. For example, most people strive to get money, but it's not the actual pieces of paper they're after, it's what money gives them. So money is the strategy to meet the need. For some, the need is purely survival: it's a way to put a roof over their heads and food in their mouths. For others, it's a way to get the respect or acceptance they want. The same goes for pornography—people are after something when they look at it."

I was starting to get it, and I was really curious now. "Got any ideas about what it might be that Garry is after?"

"I don't know about his motivation specifically, and I think it's probably different for different people. But some people might want relief from the complications of a relationship, and they still get to feel the aliveness that comes from sexual energy."

We were quiet for a while, and then he added, "But that doesn't mean porn is meeting all of Garry's needs. Often, a person will do something to try to feel better in one part of his life that has consequences for other parts of it. And then there is your side of things."

"What do you mean, my side of things?" I asked.

"Well," he said, "your pain is telling you that there are some needs that aren't being met for you when he looks at porn. If you can see those needs clearly, it will give you a greater understanding of what is so important to you."

I was hanging on to his every word. This was what I had spent weeks trawling the internet for but couldn't find: a way to understand what might be going on for the both of us. With these simple statements, I found what I was looking for and the door barring peace and understanding sprung open. There, glittering in the morning sun, was Rumi's field.

It would take a while for Garry and me to understand what this teacher meant and how we could step onto Rumi's field together, and longer yet before we could find ways to live there. This book is the story of how our insight evolved—and how we ultimately created the love we had always wanted.

chapter 2:
A Conversation
about Addiction

When I realized how much porn Garry looked at, one of my first reactions was to worry that he might be addicted to it. If he was, could we really handle the issue on our own? Were we out of our depth? This persistent question plagued me, and I finally brought it up. But the moment the word *addiction* was out of my mouth, a dark cloud moved into the room and hovered over us.

"What's up with the mood?" I asked.

"I'm not addicted, and I can stop any time," he snapped.

"Okay, then stop."

"I don't want to."

"Don't want to? Or can't?"

"Look, I want to understand what's going on for me when I look at porn. I don't want to stop doing it just because I think I'm bad for doing it." There was an edge in his voice, and his arms were crossed over his chest. Mine were too: our bodies were showing us we weren't feeling safe with one another. When I realized what I was doing, I uncrossed my arms, and then I asked him if he was feeling anxious.

"Yes," Garry said. "It scares me when I think you might want to put me in a box labeled addicted. If you decide I'm addicted, how would that increase your understanding of me? I don't believe it would. In fact, I think "addict" is just a label that prevents people from seeing what's actually going on. It doesn't say a thing about what I'm doing or why. People throw the term around, but what does it really mean?"

I thought about that for a moment. "So if I hear you right, the word addiction bothers you because it doesn't help you understand anything about yourself. Is that right?" I asked.

"Yes," he said. "I think that's true, for both the so-called addicted person and for people who hang that word on him."

I resonated with what Garry was saying, though I still felt uneasy, and thoughts of my own were percolating in the background. I remembered what my new NVC friend had said about meeting needs, connecting to what's important to us. "I don't exactly understand what's going on for you," I said, "but I keep thinking about the main idea behind nonviolent communication— that everything we do is an attempt to meet a need. Does it seem like it would be more helpful to identify what your needs are than to look at what you're doing as some kind of addiction?"

"Yes," Garry said. "Thinking of my actions as a way to fulfill needs makes more sense. I know that neither one of us fully understands what those needs are at this point, but it's a relief to think that there may be positive reasons I do what I do. If I can connect my behavior to something concrete and figure out what I'm after, I think I could get clearer, and change would be more feasible."

He rushed ahead. "The word addiction just adds another layer. See how we started talking about addiction itself rather than the issue we're struggling with? I think the word is dangerous because it's such a loaded, either/or term—either I'm addicted or I'm not—and we could spend days arguing back and forth over that. Anyway, what's the plus side? We're already trying to deal with the issue in a positive way. Would that change if we decided I was addicted?"

I was still unsure. "Well, if you are addicted, you might want to consider getting outside help from people who have had a similar experience and know more about it."

"I could do that regardless of what you call me."

I had to admit that was true. I didn't need to name his behavior anything in order for him to get help. We sat in silence for a while, each taking in what the other had said. Then he said quietly, "And Victoria ... I'm also afraid that if you decide I'm addicted, you'll treat me differently—maybe even give up on me and decide to leave."

Garry's honesty and vulnerability touched my heart. My first reaction was to reassure him, but I realized that if I were honest myself, I'd have to admit that he was probably right. I had already sensed this when I considered whether his porn use might be an addiction. If I decided it was, I probably *would* look at him differently, look at *us* differently. And as I thought this over, I realized that this attitude had its roots in my background.

My brother was an alcoholic, and our family had

been in turmoil over it for years. In and out of rehab, he tried but couldn't shake his addiction—even when his doctors told him it was going to kill him sooner rather than later. Their prophecy came true: my brother pulled his car off the road and died at age thirty-eight with a beer in his hand.

So when I thought about addiction, I imagined a life out of control and a long hard road ahead. And in this case with Garry and porn, I wasn't sure I wanted to deal with that hard road.

Garry nodded when I told him this, and I sensed his sadness.

"That's a perfect example of what I mean about this word. Nothing has changed about me from before this conversation started. I'm the same man I was an hour ago. But when you think about labeling me *addict*, suddenly our relationship might look like a road you don't want to go down."

His point made sense. "So … you want to be sure I'm seeing who you really are, not a Garry I see through addiction-colored glasses?"

"Exactly!"

BEHIND THE LABEL

Now I could hear and relate to where Garry was coming from. His point was that the word itself was static, limited—it didn't say anything about what the underlying phenomenon was. I thought about my work as an acupuncturist and the patients I had seen over the years. If they had come to me and simply said, "I'm sick," it would have been difficult to know how to work with them. But when they said something like, "I wake up in the morning and throw up, and get a headache around noon that lasts all day, and it's sharp and pounding and feels like it's right behind my eyes," it paints a picture that tells me what is actually happening.

As I contemplated the addiction label, I realized that my judgments of Garry didn't allow me to see him clearly. I was seeing him through my perceptions and fears of what it would mean if he were addicted. I understood this, but I also knew I was looking for something when I was tempted to label him as addicted: I wanted to know why *I* was so scared. And I knew there must be something more I was after, another need the label addressed. I thought for a while, and then, when it finally came to me, I told Garry.

"I guess to me, the word addiction, oddly enough, is one that represents a kind of awareness. I know that in most cases it goes the other way, like you were saying, because it's too superficial and doesn't lead to any understanding about the needs behind the behavior. But an addiction is systematic. It follows a course that involves similar stages for people. This tells me that it's tied to some reality—it's not just something we make up. So when I use the word, I'm trying to get clarity and understand what might be going on for you using that model of thinking. I care about you and want to support you, and examining a road that others have travelled is one way to do that. There are lots of communities out there that share an understanding about what's actually going on with an addicted person. I don't know if that's what you need, but I'd like to be able to talk about it as an option."

Garry's face softened. "So when you use that word, it's a way of figuring out how to best support me?"

"Yes! I want to know if you think working through this on your own is going to be enough for you, or if maybe you need the support of someone else, or a group of people who understand what goes on for people who look at porn. I can support you, but I don't know what it's like to have this strong desire to look at porn. Maybe someone who does is in a better position to help."

As I spoke, I became aware of an irony: I'd started the conversation wanting to talk about addiction, only to find it was easier to tell him what was going on for me succinctly and clearly when I didn't use the word!

Then, as if echoing my thoughts, he said, "I get where you're coming from better now, but honestly, it would have been much easier for me to hear if you had just said all that and left the label behind."

"Yeah, I think I'm getting that. But I also think there's something more I'm after when I use the word. I want to know if looking at porn is a conscious choice for you or if instead, you're in the grip of some form of compulsion that's motivated by needs you're completely unaware of."

"I'm not sure how to answer that," Garry said, "because I can only know what I know when I know it. There may be lots of things I'm not aware of that shape my choices every day. But I can say that I believe I can stop if I really want to. I wonder if part of your distress about this is that I choose to look and you want me to choose *not* to look."

I could feel the heat rising in my face. "Yeah, I think there is something about that that pisses me off. Basically, I hear you saying that *your needs* trump *my needs* — is that right?"

I could hear the anger and hurt in my voice as I spoke, but I couldn't help myself. I would almost have preferred it if he *was* addicted. Then he wouldn't keep making this *choice* that ignored *my* feelings and needs.

"No, that's not what I'm saying," Garry replied calmly. "I'm saying that until I can honestly choose to not look at porn without feeling resentful, I don't think it would be beneficial to either one of us for me to stop."

I had many thoughts going off in my head all at once. Was he just saying this as an excuse to keep looking at porn? Was my hot-tempered response somehow connected to a need I had in that moment? I was frustrated that I didn't have a handle on this concept of needs yet. What was behind my being so upset?

Then I had a flash of insight: I was sad. I really wanted to matter to Garry. Maybe that was my need. I wanted to know that he cared about how his use of porn affected me. Once I connected to that insight, something in me relaxed and I was able to hear the caring in his statement.

I sat quietly, still pondering where to go next, and realized I still had some questions about the word addiction. Finally I asked, "Is there ever a time when you think addiction can be a helpful word?"

"Maybe. I think it can be a powerful word. Like you said before, if someone is willing to accept that he's not in control of a situation, the word is a reminder of that loss of control. It could let us know that, for whatever reasons, we are powerless in relation to something. But I still think that if we use it without identifying the motivations behind the behavior we call addiction, we're not completely aware of what's going on. To me, the word doesn't contain the information we need to help us find our way."

I realized then that he wasn't saying he didn't want to talk about the issue; he was telling me he wanted things to get a lot clearer—not less so. I felt relieved, and I began to get excited.

Garry reached for my hands. "There's one thing we both know is true: there are underlying needs I can probably identify and address that relate to my looking at porn. I don't know what they are yet, but that's what I want to focus on. We're learning that this is the important information behind any desire or compulsion, right?—what needs is the person trying to meet? Would you feel comfortable if we just focused on that and see what happens without putting a label on me?"

My fear that he was addicted, somehow out of control, subsided. "Yes, I'm willing to do that," I said. Now that I trusted that he wasn't avoiding the issue out of denial—he was seriously trying to understand his own behavior in a way that included me—I felt I could relax a little. I fell silent and contemplated this.

Garry looked at me curiously and asked what I was thinking.

"I feel better," I said. "I'm happy knowing that you're willing to seriously take a look at what's going on for you. I also like seeing what's underneath the addiction word because it is so much more informative to me. I'm very grateful that we've had this conversation—I don't want to get caught up in words and concepts that limit us in any way. I'm starting to trust that we can handle this challenge ourselves now."

We ended our conversation and went about our day,

and I allowed our talk to sink into my consciousness. I felt happy and peaceful—my worldview had expanded. I was beginning to see that I didn't need to cling to alienating labels if Garry and I could keep talking like this. I wasn't completely convinced that labels weren't helpful, but somehow during our conversation I had shifted my relationship to them: the thought of dropping them no longer troubled me. Now I could see a glimmer of how focusing on needs instead could help.

As I was drifting off to sleep that night, I wondered about my brother and what it would have been like if he and I could have had a conversation like the one Garry and I had just had. I felt sad that he drank during a time when there was so little awareness—and so much stigma—concerning addiction. It didn't help him in the end, but AA has supported him and many thousands of others by bringing addiction out of isolation and into the community. I could see that our ideas about addiction were evolving and I hoped that in the future, more understanding of our underlying needs, and less labeling, would be part of that evolution.

chapter 3:
Trading Places

I was encouraged by our growing understanding, and I noticed that if I put myself in Garry's place, I felt more compassionate toward him. I wanted to feel more compassion for myself as well.

I remembered an episode of *The Oprah Winfrey Show* that dealt with people trading places with others in their lives. One story was of a husband who had a history of criticizing his wife for being tired at the end of the day when all she had to do was stay home and take care of the kids and their house. The Oprah team set up a trade: they sent the woman to a spa for several days while her husband took over her job at home.

He went crazy! He was so overwhelmed that he was unable to do even a fraction of what she did: the laundry piled up, dishes filled the sink, the beds went unmade, the kids missed a bath or two, and the man couldn't even find time to cook. He ordered pizza more than once and left the empty pizza boxes on the counters. In short, things fell apart. By the time she got back from her spa retreat, the wife found her husband a changed man. He greeted her eagerly at the door, no longer critical, instead seeing her as an omnipotent goddess. It took being in her shoes, trying to fill her role, for him to see how vital her work with the kids and their home was—and how hard it was to do.

Often, we criticize others based on our perceptions and expectations about how things *should* be when we don't have a clue about the reality of a situation. That's why I loved that episode: it demonstrated how being able to understand another person's situation can promote a powerful change in our perceptions.

So one day I had an idea. I thought it would be great to see if Garry and I could trade places. I would try to see life from his point of view, and he would try to see how life looked from mine. In some ways, just by telling each other how we felt, we had already been doing that, but this would be a more purposeful experiment. Garry agreed, and our experiment yielded some interesting results.

GARRY: *I thought this could be helpful. There was still this wall between us at times that prevented us from understanding what was going on for one another. It was as if we had two very different views of what was happening. Honestly, it was hard for me to get why porn bothered her at times because it had nothing to do with my feelings for her. I thought this would be an opportunity for us to understand each other better.*

Part One of the Experiment

Our first task was to figure out *how* we could trade places. What we came up with wasn't exactly a flat-out trade, but it allowed us to get a glimpse of each other's world.

Garry started things off by suggesting we rent porn videos so I could explore them with him and see what I thought. *Surprise, surprise!* At first I laughed, thinking it was just an excuse to look at some porn. I realized, though, that whether that was true or not, what was undeniably true of me was that I was critical of something I had little experience with myself. My exposure to porn had been limited; I had seen some magazines in my day and a few flicks here and there, but that was about it. So I agreed, and we signed up for a porn movie rental service on the internet; movies showed up a week or so after we ordered them online. The game was on!

Garry left choosing the DVDs we would watch up to me. I thought that if we were going to do this, Garry might as well get some excitement out of it, so I chose a movie I thought he would like. The first DVD arrived, and although I had some trepidation, I was curious to see how I would respond. The film opened with background music and two young women on a lawn making out, then undressing each other and having sex. I had an almost uncontrollable urge to laugh—not out of nervousness but because it was so obvious to me that these women were definitely *not* into each other.

They were acting for the cameras, and their acting was terrible. As the clothes came off, though, my mirth turned to sadness. The women had breast implants, which looked misshapen, and I wondered what their history was. I felt a mixture of sadness and anger as I stared at their altered bodies, and realized these feelings came from a deep desire to live in a world where people don't feel the need to change themselves in order to get work or be valued. And I wondered if renting this video and watching these women somehow perpetuated the belief that women had to look a certain way. It seemed similar to buying clothes made using slave labor, where the buying essentially endorses and condones the way the clothing is made.

I wondered what prompted these women to get implants. Still in the spirit of trading places, I tried to imagine some possible reasons for getting them. Maybe their breasts paid the bills, so having larger ones meant having a bigger paycheck. Maybe it was fun to have a body that turned heads. Maybe it was about going from a *nobody* to being someone special and sought after. Imagining what might be going on for them helped, but I was still sad. I thought about how much pleasure I've received from my own breasts, how sensitive they are to the touch. I had read that most women who undergo breast implant surgery lose a great deal of sensitivity, and I knew that would be a great loss for me.

Next up was a young woman imitating a child—she wore a bib and pigtails. At that point, I plunged knee-deep into painful emotions, but I wasn't able to figure out what they were. I tried to stay connected to myself so I could be clear about what was so painful, and after a bit of searching, I realized I was in the midst of a full-blown attack of shame. Here was this young woman who had a body that represented the ideal, not even close to what I looked like or what most women I knew looked like. On top of that, while she was already young, she was playing someone even younger! I was awash in thoughts about what I was *supposed* to look like, but didn't. Watching this scene reinforced ideas I'd had that women my age weren't desired—that older bodies weren't desirable. I had come to believe that older women weren't acceptable as sexual beings, while it was fine for older men to have sex with younger women.

I tried to find compassion for myself and for the way I was seeing things. Finally, I got to the bottom of it: I realized that I want to be valued—and I want all women to be valued, not just the ones who fit a very narrow mold. I want women to be treasured more for their human qualities than for their shapes and sizes. I realized, too, that I was afraid that Garry (and men in general) wouldn't be able to appreciate their real partners who might seem unappealing in comparison to these idealized women. It seemed possible that many men could be missing the gift of a real loving experience with their partners because they were blinded by these unattainable images.

I felt alone in my perceptions; it seemed to me that very few people were alarmed about this imbalanced state of affairs. I saw myself as the lone person shouting, "There's an elephant in the room!" when nobody else could see it.

I checked in with Garry to see if the movie was doing anything for him. He said that it was hard to tell because he wasn't as relaxed as he would be if he was watching it alone. He was worried about my response.

GARRY: *I felt uncomfortable watching this movie with Victoria. I couldn't let myself go into the fantasy like I do when I'm alone. One part of me was on*

guard. I worried that if Victoria was finding these
images abhorrent, what did that say about me?

Honestly, I think most men don't care about plot,
acting abilities, or what's going on for the women
on screen; they just want to look at sex. If men cared
about these qualities, they would be reflected in the
movies, because most of them are made by men for
men, and they reflect what most men want por-
trayed.

We continued to watch on the off chance that there might
be something we would both enjoy. A few minutes later
I asked Garry if he was noticing what I was sensing:
that these women were bored, uninterested in the sex.
He said he could see it but it didn't really matter, that
he was able to bypass all of that. I wondered if this was
one of those *Men Are from Mars, Women Are from Venus*
things, different and irreconcilable perceptions. The way
I saw them, each scene was more of the same: all sex, no
talking, lots of boredom. The camera rarely focused on
faces; it was mostly close-up genital shots. I couldn't get
interested. I had no connection to these images as real
people. We fast forwarded through most of the rest of
the movie, stopping only briefly along the way. To me it
seemed as if all the people in it were interchangeable.

One of the places we stopped and watched showed
a woman who, for some reason, looked to me as if she
was suffering in some way. I felt pain in my own body
while watching her. I admit that this could have been
pure projection on my part, as she was having anal sex,
and I will never really know, but her expression told me
that she was not enjoying herself. I felt very sad to be
partaking in her suffering, and at the thought that many

people might get excited by it. I wanted to cry. I was done. I didn't want to watch anymore. Garry was fine with turning it off—he wasn't enjoying himself either.

I was disappointed in the way the experiment was turning out so far. I had wanted to do this as a way to connect to what was going on for Garry but had instead ended up frustrated. I simply couldn't find it in myself to try on his perspective.

We didn't give up on our experiment, but took a few days off until I could reconnect with my desire to understand where Garry was coming from. When my enthusiasm returned, I figured there might be some older movies that had potential, and I ordered some videos from the vintage section. They arrived a week or so later, two this time. One was so old it didn't have sound, and I liked it for several reasons. First, the women were women, not girls, and they had more realistic bodies. By today's standards of beauty (what we see on TV and in the movies) these women were inadequate, but they were actually closer to what real women look like. While by no means fat, they had some flesh on them—larger thighs, rounded butts—and they weren't all the same body size and weight. They had hair and real breasts, and without the touch-up techniques available to today's moviemakers, every mole and freckle was visible, which I found refreshing. Also, I didn't pick up the pain factor I had sensed in the previous movie.

GARRY: *These movies were definitely interesting to me because I got to see my conditioning at play. I found the women in these older movies to be more accessible and friendly. They were real. But I didn't find*

them as sexually exciting because they weren't con-
sistent with the images I had been used to.

There was something else I noticed as well. Some-
times looking at the women in porn created a cycle
of pleasure and pain. The pleasure was that they
aroused me, and the pain part was that I thought
I should have a woman who looked like that, and I
didn't.

Ugh! This was exactly what had worried me. I feared that we were creating a society in which normal and real were no longer acceptable! I was still not faring well in this experiment, but I was determined to see it through.

The next movie, from sometime in the 1970s, was also pleasing to me, and I found it to be very erotic. This one was about a young woman who grows up on a farm, then leaves for the big city and becomes a call girl. The woman who starred in it appeared to be enjoying herself and the sex. Again, I have no idea if this was true. Maybe it was only that the movie actually had a semi-plot that engaged me more.

Although far from feeling the enthusiasm Garry showed for porn, I began to understand the appeal it held for him. Fueled by the movie's images, I found my-self aroused. I could see why he would want to come home after a long day at work and immerse himself in such pleasure. It was fun! For me it was kind of like watching a video game that had the effect of making the viewer feel whatever was going on in it. For days after-ward I enjoyed the lingering sexual energy I had, and I soon realized that some kinds of porn could make that energy quickly available to me.

GARRY: *Wow! When Victoria understood how this could be fun for me, I was happy that she could finally see my side of things. I was seeing something about her view as well. She wanted something to watch that had a bit of substance to it, not just sex. She wasn't opposed to sex or to seeing nude bodies—it was more about wanting to see people portrayed with reality and some dignity. The woman in this particular movie had a personality Victoria could relate to, and she wasn't altered with plastic surgery to fit the exaggerated male fantasy. If a movie had too much of those things, Victoria got upset, because seeing people as real people is very important to her.*

We continued the experiment for a while, and though we found a few films that weren't in the category of all-sex-no-plot, the ones filled solely with sex were the majority. I was disappointed with most, hoping each time to receive something I would enjoy only to find it was more of the same: all sex, no real connection. After a few more attempts, we called it quits and I happily cancelled our subscription. Garry was pleased that I had gone this far, and neither of us had remorse about any of it.

Next it was my turn. Despite the fact that I enjoyed the older movies—which surprised me—I still believed the porn industry as a whole participated in and fed a women-as-sex-objects attitude. And not just women—I believe they stereotype men as well. It seemed to me that they were repeatedly shown as thoughtless guys who didn't have a caring bone in their bodies and only valued getting off. I wanted Garry to see that even though he might not make this connection, this mind-set did exist. One part of me knew that I was trying to *educate*

Garry, probably sending a not-so-subtle message that I was right and he was wrong, but I wanted him to truly understand my concerns about the porn industry.

Through my local library I ordered a few educational DVDs: Jean Kilbourne's *Killing Us Softly 3* and *Slim Hopes*, as well as Sut Jhally's *Dreamworlds 2*. All three focused on images of women in the media and the messages they send. I thought that if we examined the messages we see every day, we could begin to understand the impact they have on how women develop in this society and how men relate to them.

My hope was that Garry would make some connections between what he was doing and the world around him. I wanted him to ask himself questions like "How does my daily consumption of these images impact me and others?" and "Is this really how I want to relate to women?" I wanted him to be able to step into what it was like to be female in a world that bombards us with media images that tell us who we *should* be and what we *should* look like. I knew that men got messages about who they were supposed to be as well, and I had compassion for that—but for now, since we were trading places, I chose the DVDs that focused on my plight.

Over the next week or two we watched all three DVDs, which showed how the media plays a central role in creating the enormous stress women and girls feel as they try to live up to an impossible image of beauty. I found that they gave voice to my feelings, putting into words what I had believed for many years: that these kinds of images limit how we see each other and do not allow us to see each other in the fullness of our beings. I have long desired to do something to change this, to confront it and deal with it on some level, and have often felt hopeless that anything I might do could help.

GARRY: *I was interested in all the presentations, but I didn't hear anything surprising. I already knew all of what they had to say. It seemed as if it was more of a clarifier than an eye opener. I had a lot of those same thoughts and ideas already, and seeing these videos helped them gel. I came away with the understanding of how important it is to address the media's stereotypical images as a social problem, not just as an individual's issue. This really is a public health issue, as many people's lives, health, and well-being are affected greatly by it.*

I also felt some hopelessness. I was so immersed in all of that programming that I almost couldn't see anything else. I guess I felt like it was too late for me—that I was so socially conditioned that I couldn't undo it, ever.

I really related to what Garry had to say. I, too, felt hopeless, and I had a deep-seated belief that I would never know freedom from my conditioned mind.

TAKING THE EXPERIMENT TO ANOTHER LEVEL

After glimpsing each other's worlds, we realized we wanted to experience them more fully, so we put our thinking caps back on and came up with part two of our experiment.

Garry and I sat down in our living room and he

closed his eyes. I asked him to imagine that the roles were reversed and that I was the one who liked to do the things he did: to imagine, for example, that Victoria, with whom Garry is now in relationship, is attracted to lots of different men, especially the younger ones. In fact, she is so attracted that she will sit for hours in front of her computer looking at images of these men.

"I stare at their genitals and imagine what it would be like to have sex with them," I said. "When you and I are out in public, I look for these young, muscled men, trying to get a glimpse of some part of them that will stimulate me. I get distracted, and at times I can't hold a conversation with you because my mind is somewhere else, wondering what they might be like in bed."

As I spoke, I sensed Garry's mounting tension. He kept his eyes closed, but his arms came up and crossed over his chest. It was a familiar gesture that usually meant he was angry, so I asked if he was. Sure enough, he was not doing well with this experiment.

"I don't want to do this anymore!"

"Why not?"

"I don't know why, but my first response is to push it away."

We continued to discuss his reaction.

"If I really see the impact this has on you," Garry began, arms still crossed over his chest, "then I feel like a schmuck, and I think I'm wrong and I should change. But I don't know how to change, and I suddenly feel like I'm at war with myself. I want to understand how this affects you, but I don't want to give in—to stop doing what you're describing—out of guilt and shame. I can't imagine you'd like me giving in under those conditions either."

His words had a strong impact on me. In his mind, he was trapped. Hearing me, taking in my pain, had only one possible outcome for him—he was a schmuck. He was right that I didn't want him to *give in*, though. That might be temporarily satisfying, but I don't believe that kind of change can last. I also wanted desperately for him to get where I was coming from. I was afraid he would pull away and we wouldn't be able to move forward. Before I could respond to what he had just said, he started speaking again.

"If I really feel your pain," he said, "I won't be able to understand why in the world you would stay in this relationship. It seems like I'm caught in a lose-lose situation. I'm not sure I want to do this anymore."

I didn't know whether to laugh or to cry in that moment. On the one hand, I was touched. I could see that by avoiding my distress, he was attempting to feel good enough about himself to justify being in a relationship with me. On the other hand, it was a strategy that would surely keep us disconnected.

"Garry," I said, "I love you very much. And I understand you have a lot of conditioning around this issue. What you're feeling is exactly what this whole experiment is for—it's for each of us to get an understanding of the other person's world. You're starting to see and feel my perspective, and that's the point. I want you to be able to see my side as well as your own—and I want to understand yours. I'm sorry if I've contributed to that being difficult for you in any way, and I know that there are still times when I want to blame you, but I'm really trying hard not to do that. Do you think it would be possible for you to just feel what it's like to be me without blaming yourself?"

"Maybe another time," he said. "I think I'm done for now, though. I need some time to think about things."

I could tell that Garry was hurting so badly he couldn't hear me any longer, and I knew it was best to just let things settle for a while. Over the next couple of days, I took time to examine my true intentions for these experiments—and what I learned was revealing.

Although my intention was to explore both sides, I found that I still wanted to blame him, and my *secret hope* was that Garry would finally realize he was wrong and want to change. There were times when it was very difficult to stay connected to how much I loved him because I was so frightened that he wouldn't change. I desperately wanted to find a way to deal with my fears by placing the responsibility for them on Garry and making him admit that his actions were hurting me. I had been having visions of him transformed, like that guy on *Oprah*, or like Ebenezer Scrooge upon waking from his ghostly visits. I'd pictured Garry begging forgiveness from me and all the women he consumed for his pleasure. I wanted him to never look at another magazine or movie containing naked women again.

I brought my insights to Garry.

"I've realized that there have been times throughout this experiment when I came into it with the intention to prove you wrong. Right now I feel really bad about that. What I really want is to create a safe space where we can talk about what's going on without any fear of being judged by each other."

He looked pleased. "Thanks, Victoria. I've had some of that proving-you-wrong energy myself at times. When you bring it out into the open like that, it makes it so much easier for me to not want to do it anymore either. How about we start fresh?"

DIFFERENT POINTS OF VIEW

In our newfound place of connection, we took up our experiment again. This time, Garry wanted to go first. I sat down, took a deep breath, and closed my eyes. Garry began to talk, speaking as though I was the one experiencing what he described.

"From a very young age, you are encouraged to look at women," he began. "This encouragement is everywhere: movies, television, magazines, and music. You hear it from schoolmates and all the men in your life. As you grow up, women in the media look back at you, putting effort into trying to be sexy and seemingly wanting you to look. You find them plastered on gigantic billboards; they fill movie screens and prance around in music videos. They all seem to want to be sexy, to be seen, to be looked at in a sexual way. Why else would they be doing what they constantly do? What you learn is that women *want* to be seen as sexual objects, that they crave it."

I let that sink in. I had two reactions at the same time to what he was saying. One was that I imagined how hard it would be for a young boy who had been given no other perspective to think any differently, and how this thinking had been reinforced with ever-present images throughout adulthood. My other response was to reject everything he was saying. If I didn't, I thought I would have to buy the perspective that women want to be seen as sexual objects—and if that was true, then the very conditions that had led me to my painful quandary would never change.

Now the roles were reversed. Just as Garry had only a few days prior, I was the one who felt trapped. I had these two reactions battling in me, and I was afraid the battle would take over and I would lose my chance to see what was going on for Garry. For the moment anyway, I chose to come back to my dilemma later and again turned my attention to what Garry was saying.

"Now imagine you're surrounded by all of those messages," he continued, "and then you get different, conflicting messages from other sources—like your church and your parents—that sexual feelings and sexual desires are bad. It's like seeing big, delicious cookies through a glass cookie jar and then you're told that you can't take the lid off. Suddenly that cookie jar becomes everything in the world to you. How do you feel finding yourself in that situation?"

I didn't even have to think about my answer. "Like you—angry and confused as I receive so many mixed messages from all angles. One part of my world is saying this is what you should want and desire, and the other part says, 'No.' I want relief from the conflict these mixed messages create. I also want some understanding for how difficult this might be for me and for men in general."

"Right," Garry said. "That's exactly it. It's as if I'm being criticized for something I've been told is okay and have been encouraged to do my whole life. Looking at women in a sexual way has become an automatic, unconscious response, and it's not an easy thing to stop or change. A part of me understands why you're so upset, because from my perspective it seems that the media is all about promoting porn—they use sexual images everywhere. Yet if I follow where that promotion ultimately leads and look at porn, or even look at women on the street, suddenly it's not okay. This is a huge mixed message—I feel really confused."

I was enjoying our connection, but I had a growing awareness of an emotion percolating in the background, making its way forward into my consciousness. It had something to do with the fact that, now that I was able to see his side of things, I didn't know what to do with my pain. For so long it had had a place—a source—and that place was with men. Suddenly I saw that I now wanted to transfer it over to women.

"Right now I'm feeling really pissed off at myself—and all women," I told Garry, "because of how we perpetuate being seen as sex objects by focusing so much of our attention on beauty. How many times have I dressed to be sexually attractive and then been angry when someone whistled or stared at my breasts? We're so steeped in our own oppression that we've come to support it and believe in it. We can't see anything different. It reminds me of a quote by Harriet Tubman, 'I freed thousands of slaves; I could have freed thousands more if they had known they were slaves.'"

Garry listened quietly, then said, "You know, I think we're all slaves—you, me, everybody—as long as we stay disconnected from ourselves and just do things mindlessly without understanding what's truly motivating our actions."

I had to agree with him.

We could have stopped there, because we both were so connected in that moment. But there were things I wanted him to know about myself and my side of this.

We lay down on the bed side by side and closed our eyes. As I began to speak, I tried to remember my intention to see each other's point of view and not make Garry wrong.

"Imagine that you're female and growing up in a world where males are granted the right to see women as objects—to be looked at and valued by the size and shape of their bodies, not their human qualities. You hear messages from men that dissect women into parts, like 'I'm a leg man' or 'I'm an ass man.' Restaurants like Hooters are named for the breasts that will wait on you, not for the food. Most of the images of women you see in magazines and movies and on billboards are devoid of any real personalities because their worth is only in what they look like. You notice that the images men are most attracted to are images of perfection and youth, which gives you the message that in order to be valued and loved you must maintain this standard. So you begin a lifelong pursuit of trying to be what men want. You develop strategies like dieting and dressing in the right clothing in an attempt to be valued. But those strategies come from your sense of deficiency, and instead of giving you a deeper, richer sense of self, they reinforce the idea that you aren't enough."

Garry was silent, but I sensed he was following me.

"Now imagine that you have a strong desire to live differently. You realize how influenced you've been by these images and how you've mistaken them for reality. You can see that you're not nourishing yourself or what really matters to you. So you decide to create a world in which you're not faced with these images and impossible ideals on a daily basis. You begin to feel better about yourself.

"And then you find yourself in a relationship with a person who spends a lot of his energy in search of images of idealized bodies. This person loves to look at women as objects of desire: the very thing you've striven to get away from. The women he likes are young, thin, and a specific kind of idealized beauty, and he sometimes sits for hours at a time looking at them. They are not you, and bear no relation to what you look like or who you are ... and he desires them.

"Can you tell me how you would feel if this was you?"

Garry lay quietly for a moment—no crossed arms, no anger, his eyes closed.

Softly, he spoke as if he were in my place. "I would feel so sad. I want to know that I'm valued by my partner. I imagine how good it would be if I could trust that my partner is present and committed to me. And I want my partner to care about the same things I do. I would really enjoy knowing that my partner cares about the quality of life he brings into the home and the relationship."

I started to cry. He really had understood it. He got what I was saying, and he connected with how it was for me. Garry opened his eyes and held my gaze.

"I can see how my looking at porn could be a constant reminder of the pain of thinking you are never enough."

We lay together for a long while, quietly holding each other. Like the newly awakened husband on the *Oprah* show, we were both changed, each looking at the other in a new light. As I bathed in our connection, it dawned on me that what I had been wanting for our relationship all along was exactly this: to see and hear each other clearly. Nothing less would do.

chapter 4:
Changes and Choices

Even though Garry and I were making some progress by talking, and we were finding lots of ways to connect with one another, I was still tormented. It felt like things were moving too slowly: Garry was still looking at porn, and I was still in pain. What did it mean that I stayed with him under these circumstances?

What bothered me most was that despite the great start we'd made, he was still making choices about how to live his life that ran counter to some of my most important values, and I just didn't know how I could live with that. When I was in this emotional cycle it was devastating. One moment I'd experience a sudden rush of soft and tender feelings toward Garry, and the next moment my anguish would return: just as suddenly, I would become convinced that I didn't want to—that I couldn't—live with so much distress.

I was often agitated and dogged by persistent questions. I was consumed with wanting to know what was in my best interest: go or stay? Was what he was doing generally accepted male behavior? Was I overreacting? Was I supporting his behavior by staying? If I left before

I understood our actions and reactions, would I come to regret it? And more: I questioned whether I was in integrity with myself. Did staying mean I didn't respect myself?

I wanted to know why this deep conflict was in my life and what I was supposed to learn from it.

I picked up a book called *Deal Breakers: When to Work on a Relationship and When to Walk Away*, by Dr. Bethany Marshall. Dr. Marshall defined *deal breaker* in ways I found helpful: "A deal breaker is a character flaw or emotional stance that significantly deteriorates the quality of a relationship," "... [it's] not a deal breaker unless it destroys something precious to you," and "... deal breakers undermine the very conditions that make it possible to love."

These ideas all spoke to one of my strongest beliefs: there is no reason to stay in *any* situation that doesn't support my well-being. And I knew that if I stayed in a relationship that wasn't in my best interest, it certainly wouldn't be in Garry's best interest either.

Even with these insights as my guide, it was challenging to figure out what to do—a gut-wrenching period for me. Which road would lead me toward strengthening myself? Yes, I could leave, but I didn't want to miss an opportunity to see where this love could take us, or to understand both Garry and myself more deeply. Could I accomplish these things and still be in integrity with myself? I also knew that if I stayed and continued to feel so resentful, it would probably surface as sarcasm, punishment, shame, or blame and create a toxic environment for both of us.

In this chapter I further describe this struggle and how I came to the decision I ultimately made. Garry was clear: he wanted me to stay and he wanted to work on the relationship. Although he felt anxious knowing how ambivalent I was, he allowed me the space to make my own decision.

The choice of whether we remained together would be mine.

A FALSE START: DEMANDING CHANGE

When I expressed my anguish to a friend, she said, "You do have another choice besides staying and living with porn, or going. Tell him that this is unacceptable behavior for you, and if he doesn't stop, you're out of there. It's as simple as that." Power surged through me at the thought. Yes! I could lay down the law, and if he really loved me he would stop. Making Garry change to show his love was like making him prove he cared—if he stopped looking at porn, then he must love me. And this means of getting my way was very seductive. It was familiar, the kind of threat I was brought up with: "Do this or else" was a phrase I knew well.

I felt empowered for the rest of the day. Why hadn't I thought of this before? It made so much sense to let him know that I just didn't want to deal with this issue anymore—and that if he didn't stop, I was out the door. It would be simple and effective and would shift the responsibility onto his shoulders. I could simply react to his decision and then make my own.

By the time Garry came home, my heart was pounding in anticipation. I started speaking as soon as he walked in the door.

"Garry, we have to talk. I just can't stand the tension anymore, and how upset I get over your looking at porn. It just hurts too much. So I'm asking you, for the sake of our relationship, to give it up."

Garry stared at me, his expression blank. I swallowed hard, then rushed ahead. "Of course, if looking at porn is more important to you than I am, I'll have to accept that. But just know that if that's the case, I won't be able to stay. That's the bottom line.

"So ... will you give it up?"

I waited for his reaction, my body tense. After what seemed like hours, he replied simply, "Okay."

That was it? It was that easy? It wasn't exactly an enthusiastic response, but he had agreed. I sighed with relief, not quite believing how well things had worked out.

I should have known better. From the work I had been doing with Nonviolent Communication, I knew conceptually that making such demands probably wouldn't get me what I wanted. I was soon to discover firsthand that it absolutely does not work—and why.

Garry stopped looking at porn, but immediately the energy in our relationship shifted. We had less intimacy, we talked less, and our contact was routine—there was no real connection behind it. Garry took on a kind of zombie aspect, as if he was there but not *there.* I didn't recognize the reason right away—I felt anxious but couldn't put my finger on why. About a week later, it occurred to me that the frosty atmosphere had blown in just after my ultimatum. I asked him what was bothering him, and he admitted to having been angry ever since.

"You delivered an ultimatum without any care about what was going on for me. It didn't seem like you gave a damn about what I thought. You just made a decision with no concern at all for my feelings."

"I gave you a choice. You could have chosen not to stop."

"God, Victoria. What kind of choice is that? I love you, and you threaten to walk out if I don't do what you want! Give me a break! You ask me to stop looking at porn when I don't have any understanding about why I feel so compelled to look at it. If I banish a part of myself just to make you happy, do you really think it will be a deep, lasting change? This week I've only been doing what you asked to please you, and honestly, I'm already resenting the hell out of you for asking this of me. It reminds me of my childhood—if I didn't do what I was told, I was punished. Well, I'm not a kid, and I don't appreciate your treating me like one!"

He broke off abruptly, laughing now. "Actually, I guess I'm acting like one right now."

I was terribly confused. I knew exactly what he was talking about—I had also grown up with ultimatums as a child, and I had despised them. Yet I still wanted to be able to make demands on Garry. I yearned for the power to make him change just by saying "Do it." I had so wanted my fear and confusion to cease that I had seized on this demand as my best hope. Only now did I realize that the method I'd chosen wasn't going to achieve that goal, and I knew that I needed to better understand what was happening between us, so for the sake of clarity I checked in with him by asking a few questions.

"Are you saying that you want to feel like you're in a partnership with me instead of what feels like me just telling you what to do? Do you want more consideration for how you're feeling about all of this?"

"Yes! I don't want to feel like I'm being coerced into something, and worry that I'll lose you if I don't comply."

I felt a glimmer of hope and started to cry. "I wanted all of this to go away. I wanted you to show your love for me by choosing me instead of the porn."

He took me in his arms. "Victoria, I'm showing you how much I love you by telling you who I am and being as honest as I can with you. I have a long history of doing things for others while resenting it. I don't want to live my life that way anymore. If I'm going to change, it must be for my own reasons. I'm afraid if I try to just stop without understanding what's going on for me, it will be destructive—for me, and for our relationship in the long run."

As soon as he said those words, I heard the truth in them, and I relaxed. We ended the conversation with a better comprehension of each other's perspective, and the distance that had been hanging between us all week disappeared. For the moment, I didn't feel scared or insecure about his looking at porn.

And I thought that feeling would last. But all my questions crept back over the next week, and once again I found myself back in that familiar place: he was still looking at porn, and I was still in conflict. Could I live with Garry and porn? I didn't think so, yet I didn't know how I could change the situation in a way that didn't demand the change.

In my heart of hearts, what I really wanted was for him to stop looking at porn because he had decided to do so ... and I wanted his reasons to be along the lines of "I love Victoria, she's more important to me than porn, so I'll quit." I wanted him to come to this decision on his own, without feeling pressure from me.

I realized that when I had demanded Garry comply with what I wanted, I had set us up for failure. As I could have predicted if I'd fully thought it through, he reacted with resistance to "Do this, or else!" Most of us would. When I tried to force him to make a choice he didn't want to make, I made it difficult for him to choose options that would benefit us both. I was essentially saying, "I am in pain—now fix it!" When he heard that message, he believed he was responsible for it, and he complied, but underneath he resented the ultimatum. He believed he didn't have a choice.

But what I really wanted was for Garry to so greatly value what was important to me that he would, in fact, make a choice—one that supported me. Was there a way I could get him to understand so that he would actually want to change? I recalled the NVC idea that people only act to meet their needs, and I thought that I might be able to show Garry that if he changed in the ways I wanted him to, he could actually meet his own needs. Here's an example of what I mean. One reason I wanted Garry to stop looking at porn was because I wanted his attention to shift to me. If I could get him to see how making this shift would meet his needs, too, then he might choose to do it.

I liked this idea, but I knew that acting upon it wasn't going to be easy: I knew I still didn't fully grasp the concept of needs. I decided to just do the best I could by speaking from my heart again. Garry willingly listened as I explained that figuring out why I was so upset about porn was difficult, and that I wanted to share some ideas with him. I took a deep breath and began.

"First, I want to know that I'm number one in your life. I want to feel secure in that knowledge. I want to have a sense that I'm cherished and that you desire me not only physically but as someone you want to spend time with. I want to feel secure that as we get older you will appreciate my age and what comes with it and not be turned off because it's not like what you're used to looking at in pictures."

At this point tears were welling in my eyes, but I plowed ahead.

"I know that there is no such thing as lasting security—change is the nature of life—but I guess I want at least some relative security, and to know that we share the same values. I want to be able to trust our relationship enough to just let go and reveal myself to you with no fear.

"For some reason—and this is when I start to feel confused—when I see you looking at porn so frequently, I don't feel secure. Everything I want from you seems to go out the window. That's the part of me that wants you to stop. I believe with all my heart that if I really feel secure in our relationship, I'll want to be here with you and will open up more, which in turn will give you the kind of security I think you probably want as well."

It felt as if I wasn't getting my point across ... I wasn't even exactly sure what my point was—it was as though I was circling it but couldn't quite reach it. I paused to check in with him and ask how he was with hearing me. He took a deep breath, too, and jumped in—as fearfully as I had. "Well, I'm a little confused, and a little panicked. Part of me thinks I have to do something that will make you feel secure, and I don't know what to do. It seems that no matter how much I tell you I love you,

you can't hear me. Another part of me is struggling to understand what it is that you do need. Do you need for me to love you more?"

For some reason, I was uncomfortable and confused hearing those words. "No, that's not it," I said.

"Well, what is it then?"

"I was hoping that if you could understand what was behind my desire to want you to stop looking at porn, then you would want to stop. I guess I just want to know that you really understand what's important to me, and I want you to want to support those things."

Now Garry looked less confused. "Oh, okay. So ... do you want some confirmation that I understand what it is that's important to you?"

"Yes, I think that would help."

Garry took a minute to reflect on what I had said, then began, "I think one thing I heard you say is important is security. You want to know that your well-being is important to me. Is that right?"

"Yes, that's part of what I want. I also want to know that my body stimulates you and turns you on, not someone else's body you project onto me. I want us to feel good about meeting our needs within this relationship. When I see you looking to pornography to meet your needs, I worry that there may be something we're not addressing between us. I know you were looking at porn long before I came along, but I'm concerned that it's getting in the way of us having the kind of intimacy I long for."

"What kind of intimacy are you looking for?"

It was a good question, and the answer came to me clearly. "The kind that touches me at my core, Garry, and that helps me see my true self, beyond the self that

I show to the world. I want a relationship that supports me in being more alive and aware. I would like to create a place for us to feel safe to reveal ourselves even in the face of our vulnerability. I want the aliveness that comes from really being seen and heard by each other. That's what I want with you."

Garry paused to take this in, working something over in his mind. Then a look of wonder crossed his face.

"I'm realizing that I actually want that kind of intimacy too. This is the only relationship I've been in where I've felt safe enough to want to reveal myself, and it feels really good. And that's why I want to be completely honest with you. I know you don't always enjoy what I tell you, but I can see that you take it in and respect that I've told you the truth. That really encourages me to open up even more."

Wow! Hope welled up in my heart. I realized that his looking at porn was painful for me because it seemed to get in the way of the kind of quality I wanted in our relationship. But now, when I heard that he wanted the same things I did, my fear diminished. This was the key I had been looking for. If I could show Garry that his not looking at porn could support our intimacy, then surely he would know that stopping would meet needs of his own. I took the plunge.

"I really want to nurture the intimacy in our relationship, and it sounds like you do too, so I would like to ask you to stop looking at porn for a while. I'd like for us to see what would happen if you just looked to this relationship to meet the needs you've been trying to meet with porn. Are you uncomfortable with this idea?"

This felt so much better to me than had my previous demand. I could ask it in a way that revealed how the change could make life more wonderful for the both of us. Garry was quiet, looking thoughtfully at me as he reflected. Finally he said, "The best way I can be intimate with you right now is to tell you that I am not ready to stop looking at porn. I want you to know that I care about how this affects you—I do—but if I stop without understanding it, and only because I think I should, I will be hurting us in the long run. I don't yet understand why I like to look at it so much, and I need some time to figure it out. I suspect that there are lots of reasons, maybe some positive and maybe some not. But I won't know until I can see it all more clearly. We've already seen that trying to force change doesn't work. It won't be real and I'll just end up resenting you for it."

Garry continued, his voice soft. "I want you to know that I am actually aware of what I'm doing in a way I've never been before. I would like it if you could be patient with me as I find my own way. I know you're trying to figure out whether or not you can live with this in your life, and it's scary to think that you're ready to bolt at any moment if something doesn't change, but I figure we have a far greater chance of being successful as a couple if you know what's true for me than we would if I did or said something just to put a Band-Aid on our trouble."

He paused, and I waited quietly. Then he went on: "What I really want is to understand this. I want to be free. I want to be free to look, but I also want to be free not to look, which hasn't felt like a possibility until recently. I've been in rebellion mode for so long that it's become a kind of prison—one I made myself. Until recently, I didn't see that. Something powerful is happening in my life, and it's because of our relationship. I'm becoming much more aware of what goes on inside me, and I want to continue that, but I need to know that you're going to be here solidly, not with one foot out the door. I want to understand what I'm doing, not just quit it because someone says I should. I want this not just for me—I want to understand because I care about you and our relationship."

Even though it wasn't exactly what I had hoped to hear, Garry's words calmed some anxious part of me. The truth I heard in his words told me that I could trust them—that I could trust him. Our conversation was alive with integrity and authenticity that are born out of honesty, and from this emerged a vibrant sense of choice that opened us to freedom. The resulting intimacy was palpable. I was getting exactly what I wanted: Garry was telling me that even though he was scared I would leave, he wanted to be honest with me and with himself. He was saying "no" to my request that he stop viewing porn but "yes" to the intimacy I wanted. I could see that he was being honest with himself, and with clarity he'd never had before. While in our earlier conversation I had heard the words I wanted to hear—that he would stop looking at porn—they'd left me feeling anxious and had brought tension and resentment into our relationship. This time, although his answer was no, his words were deeply satisfying. In fact, they allowed me to look more closely at myself.

I wanted to bring the same quality of honesty to myself and the relationship, and I knew it was time to get clear as to what my truth was and decide whether to stay or go.

DECISION-MAKING TIME

Uncertainty plagued me, and I sought the advice of the same NVC trainer who had started us on this path. He asked me to look at the needs I would meet with the choice I made, and suggested it was likely that if I stayed I would meet one set of needs, and if I left I would meet another. To get me started, he gave me a less charged example than the big decision before me: if my girlfriends call and want a girls' night out but Garry and I have a stay-at-home popcorn and movie night planned, each option would meet a different set of needs. Staying home might give me the rest or intimacy with Garry I wanted, while joining my friends might meet my needs for play and friendship. Being so explicit about my needs would allow me to weigh each one carefully to see which needs were more important at the moment. The same concept could work for our relationship.

Stay or go; that was the question. This method to get at an answer was simple, and I liked that. I was to ask myself a series of questions about my choices, and check to see how I felt: what my heart told me when I thought about a particular idea. Did it hurt to think about making a particular choice? Did it feel exciting, difficult, or frightening? I could look at each idea and potential choice I might make without having to decide to take action right away, and I would be able to get in touch with my feelings about each one.

Here's how I responded to the questions:

Leaving

When I asked myself how I felt about leaving, I felt some relief in my body, a feeling of ease and peace. It came when I imagined no longer having to deal with porn in my life. I liked the idea of living in my own safe and comfortable space, free of painful triggers and strife.

Leaving also seemed like a way I could make sure I didn't fall into my old pattern of changing myself to please others. It would support me in being true to myself.

When I reminded myself that I didn't have to stay, I felt like I had more choice, and this supported me in being in my own power. And when I took a step back, I saw that in the big picture, I didn't believe that porn was a beneficial strategy to meet needs, and this meant that leaving would be a way I could be in harmony with my values and in alignment with my integrity.

My last consideration—but by no means the least— was that it was very important for me to value myself and to be valued. Leaving was one way to do that; by saying "no" to porn, I could say "yes" to myself.

I sat for a couple of days with all of these responses to the idea of leaving, giving them room to settle in. Then, when I was ready, I switched hats and asked myself how I felt about the choice to stay.

Staying

I sensed that there was more to this choice than I could comprehend. If I stepped back from my own triggers of pain, I was left with a strong curiosity about the connections between Garry's looking at porn and my own issues involving sexuality. I also really wanted to know Garry and what was motivating his actions.

Through this struggle in our relationship, I was discovering a new level of intimacy that was about seeing Garry just as he was—and revealing who I truly was. This depth of intimacy scared me, but it also thrilled me because of the aliveness that came with it.

While I could imagine how easy and peaceful life would become if I left, I could also imagine finding those qualities if I stayed. When I thought of the possibility that Garry and I could use getting to the root of this issue as a way to see ourselves and each other more clearly, I no longer had the sense that I would have to manipulate my environment as a way to stay safe.

Finally, I realized I had a choice about staying as well. In fact, I didn't just have one choice—to stay. I realized that I had many choices about *how* I wanted to be within the relationship if I stayed.

As I sat with these insights, feeling into each and every aspect of all the choices I could make, things started to get clearer for me. Even though I was feeling pain about porn, I was also learning and growing in ways I couldn't have imagined otherwise. Now, instead of measuring my life by my comfort level, I was shifting to a different kind of measuring system consisting of qualities of life I valued and wanted to nurture. I liked the possibilities I sensed in shifting from "Garry is the source of my pain" to "I'm clearer about the quality of life I want to create for both of us."

I also saw that Garry wasn't just "a guy who looked at porn." He was in fact multidimensional, with many characteristics I loved and cherished. It was only when

I was hurting that I focused on this one aspect of him. For the most part, my interactions with Garry were filled with kindness and consideration, and I was often in awe of his generosity of spirit and affectionate nature. And I found his willingness to communicate honestly about this complex and often confusing issue deeply fulfilling.

I remembered a passage in *Deal Breakers*, where Dr. Bethany Marshall offered "a new and empowering definition of a deal breaker: A deal breaker is a negative or standstill arrangement that, once recognized, can be used as a tool for positive change." Her words gave me hope that we could use this challenge as an opportunity for growth.

The bottom line was that I wanted to see this thorny issue through with Garry. I knew that if I walked away I would always wonder how life could have been were we to dig into the depths of what was behind our behaviors and choices. We had missed that opportunity years before when we decided to go our separate ways, and I had some regret over all the time we had lost together. I wanted to see what it was that had kept us connected and called us back to one another after such a span of years.

I decided to stay.

GARRY: *"Once Victoria made her decision I could feel the difference in both of us. Knowing that she was no longer on the fence, I was more open to exploring. I felt her commitment to the relationship, and that gave me the confidence to open up to her and to us*

even more. Her decision to stay didn't mean that our struggle disappeared. In fact, it was actually more like it was just beginning. But because I knew she was here to stay, I was much more hopeful that we could ride it out."

We were on our way.

chapter 5:
The Needs of Both Sides

My decision to stay shifted the energy between Garry and me. Now that I no longer had one foot out the door, we had a greater sense of trust and safety, and that made it easier to open up to each other and more fully reveal our vulnerable, tender places. We decided the time was right to figure out just what these needs were that supposedly motivated everything we did, so we committed ourselves to exploring them.

We both still found it difficult to grasp the concept fully: our needs seemed elusive, and we equated them with something negative. We attributed this partly to the fact that, in our culture, we aren't trained to think in terms of needs. We struggled with the word—it brought up visions of being dependent upon others: needy and clingy. It hinted of helplessness, immaturity, and selfishness. We thought *need* was at odds with *independent* and *strong*—qualities we both had come to believe we should exhibit. Adding to our confusion, we had both learned from an early age to focus on others instead of ourselves, so it was difficult to acknowledge that we even had needs, let alone recognize what they were.

Through practicing Nonviolent Communication, we were able to begin unraveling the mystery of needs. In this chapter I will share with you some of what we learned about them as I describe how we began to identify our own.

In NVC, needs are far from selfish and they do not reflect dependence on others. In fact, needs represent our core values and our deepest human longings. We all share basic survival needs—such as for air, food, and water—but we also share other important needs like connection, intimacy, freedom, autonomy, and choice (to name just a few). While we all have the same needs, we place different significance on each need based on our individual character. For example, where intimacy is a very important need for me, it might be less so for someone else; autonomy may be of greater importance to you than it is to me. In other words, the priorities placed on different needs vary for each person. (See the appendix for a complete list of the needs we all share.)

Because the word *need* can conjure up negative connotations, people may respond with more receptivity when we substitute synonyms such as *long for, hope for, value,* or *want*. Some examples are "I value kindness and honesty in my relationship" or "I want, hope, or long for kindness and honesty in my relationship" instead of "I need kindness and honesty in my relationship."

I studied NVC with Robert Gonzales, who said, "Needs are just the basic life energy expressing through our actions and words, seeking fulfillment." Because needs seek expression through action, we sometimes confuse a person's actions with the need he or she is trying to meet. Say, for example, a person buys a new car. The purchase of that car is simply the action, or strategy, he carries out in order to meet a need. His need may be for freedom, or it may be for survival: he might seek transportation to enjoyable events to meet his need for fun, or to a job so he can provide food and shelter for himself and his family. The needs are very different, but the action taken to meet them is the same—buying a car. Another person might buy an expensive car hoping to meet her need to be valued, believing that others will think more highly of her if she has a nice car. Again, different need, same strategy or action.

Relating to ourselves and others at the level of needs required a shift in consciousness for us—and it wasn't easy. Before we embarked on this exploration of needs, we had related to people based on whether or not we agreed with the *strategies* they used to meet their needs. We judged others, and ourselves, by what we believed was right and wrong—a dominant and pervasive perspective in our culture. We hadn't been able to see past people's actions to connect to the needs underlying them—what they were after when they did what they did. As we began to consider other people's behavior through the lens of needs, we were able to look beyond our own actions as well, and start to understand the needs we were attempting to fulfill.

This was when life started to get really interesting and informative.

GARRY: *When Victoria first explained the concept that everything we do is motivated by our desire to meet needs within ourselves, I wasn't sure what that meant. But something about it intrigued me, so I stayed open to hearing more about it.*

I had never wanted to explore why I liked to look at porn, for two reasons. First, conventional belief is that desiring porn is just the way men are, some mysterious thing about being male—I figured I'd never understand it, so why bother to try? That was an easy and unchallenging belief. Second, I didn't want to face the thought that there might be something wrong with me and that this desire for porn was beyond my control. Would I end up like a man I once knew, dying a lonely death, a computer loaded with porn his only legacy? This was so scary for me that I just did not want to go there. I had found it difficult to talk to Victoria about my attraction to porn because I was afraid she would believe, or I would have to admit, that she was with someone who was damaged beyond redemption.

With this new framework of needs I began thinking that maybe I could go there after all. Maybe I would be able to understand my attraction to pornography if I could figure out the needs I was trying to meet with it. Maybe I would be able to see and understand myself in a way that would alleviate the fear that I was some kind of monster. This was what motivated me to finally open up and explore my desire for porn.

Still, I was confused. What the heck were these needs she was talking about? Did I even have any? And if I did, that meant Victoria had needs too, and I wasn't sure I wanted to hear about them because I could already sense myself feeling responsible for them. Did I really want to open this can of worms?

I knew that if I was going to venture down this path with her, I would have to understand more clearly what needs were.

DISCOVERING OUR NEEDS

As I mentioned, NVC offers a list of all basic human needs, which you will find in the appendix. We looked them over in an attempt to figure out what was going on for us, trying each one on to see if it fit. When we identified one that matched our own circumstance, we each experienced a sense of it fitting like a puzzle piece, followed by an expansion of awareness. And when we expressed our needs to each other, we were suddenly able to understand where the other person was coming from.

Garry was first to come up with some insights about the needs he thought motivated his behavior.

GARRY: *Figuring out what needs I was trying to meet by looking at porn was downright challenging. It took me weeks before I could even come up with a few ideas, and it was even longer before I could get to the more significant ones.*

There was something about the need for acceptance that seemed important to me. When I'm in the world of porn, I'm not a deviant anymore, I'm part of a community of like-minded people who think any desire is okay. This is a relief. It's also a place where people play with their fantasies. It brings out my own sense of play and creativity, and helps me to connect with parts of myself that are normally hidden. I guess I would say that porn helps me be more authentic in some ways, and more self-connected. In the world of porn I can be seen for who I am: someone who is interested in looking at sex.

Even though I still had some concerns, fear, and even anger when Garry shared these insights, I was surprised at how much his revelations softened my feelings toward him. When he was able share himself and open to his own vulnerabilities, it invited me to be open as well. The process helped me to see him as the person he was, not just a reflection of my fears.

It took time and many conversations to work through and identify our needs. I'm not sure we will ever be able to connect to all of our needs, but eventually we were fairly satisfied that we had come to understand ourselves and each other more fully. This was profound, but it wasn't magic: it wasn't as if once we identified our needs we were able to relax, or that it fixed everything. Needs often get restimulated, or they come up again in a different context, and we have to tend to them every time they come up. As a teacher of mine once said, "Life isn't a one-walk dog; you have to keep taking it out again and again." The same goes for needs: after all, they are expressions of life.

Garry continued to explore the needs he was meeting by looking at porn, and eventually he came up with even more.

GARRY: *Once I put my attention on needs, I began to see more and more of my actions through that perspective. I thought about how my needs could have been formed by my past — and it started to make sense.*

I grew up in a family where expressing needs for affection, attention, and love was uncomfortable and discouraged. My parents rarely expressed any emotion other than anger openly. I found out later that my dad wanted out of the marriage but had agreed to stay until my brothers and I were grown and out of the house. His actions were not a role model for love or intimacy in a relationship, only responsibility.

We didn't talk about sex in our household, and the church we belonged to had a fire-and-brimstone attitude toward it, which made it that much more difficult to understand the feelings I had as I grew up. I learned to hide parts of myself as a way to cope. On those rare times when I did reveal my need for affection or attention, I was told it wasn't okay ("Don't be a sissy, be a man!") and I learned that it wasn't safe to expose my inner world to others.

Because I had learned that lust and desire were not traits of a good person, I tried to hide those parts of myself. I felt conflicted much of the time, but when I was in the world of porn those feelings were accepted, and for that time I could accept them in myself.

I was in a conundrum when it came to relationships. Somewhere along the line I picked up the belief that women and sex were the goal, the secret to happiness, and I wanted them. I also feared women because, in my mind, I gave them power over my happiness. So I ended up hiding parts of myself to make sure they loved me. Not feeling safe enough to expose my true self and my feelings, I found it difficult to maintain a lasting relationship. But in the world of porn I could have a pseudo-relationship while not having to hide parts of myself. What a relief this was! The imaginary women in porn accepted me for who I was, lust and all. They didn't judge or criticize. It was a place where I had the safety and protection I needed to accept those parts of myself that I thought were unacceptable.

But all of this hiding and telling myself that I wasn't okay had a deadening effect on me. And although I had jobs that paid good money, they were routine, and I thought of myself as just a part in the machine. Sometimes it seemed I was on an endless treadmill going nowhere.

But in the world of porn I could come alive. I felt the exhilaration of sexual energy pulsing through me with no fear or anxiety holding me back. I'm not sure what that need would be called, but if there is a need for feeling alive, that's what this was. Interestingly, there were times when I'd quit work to go sailing for a few months, and I got the same sense of freedom and being in touch with life—and I didn't even think about porn when I was out there on the water.

Each time Garry identified the needs he was meeting by looking at porn and shared them with me, some of my rigidity and agitation subsided and my connection with him strengthened. It didn't mean that those feelings didn't return, but in those moments I was able to experience what it was like to not have to draw a line between us or choose a side—right or wrong, good or bad. When

I connected to needs, there *were* no sides, only a feeling of being connected to something more real.

When I was able to sweep aside thoughts of right and wrong, I imagined Garry as a young boy with a healthy sexual appetite, experiencing all the feelings of lust, desire, and curiosity about sex that any young person feels, yet constrained in an environment where he didn't feel safe expressing any of it. I imagined how he learned to tamp it down, to not express it outwardly, to not share and not ask questions—and I could guess how uncomfortable that must have been for him. I began to see how porn could feel like a safe place where he could find acceptance for all of those confusing feelings, and how it might facilitate a connection to himself in a way he hadn't been able to figure out in the real world. I could easily see how attractive it might be, this carefree place filled with fun and excitement.

I shared these thoughts with Garry so he could see the effect his words were having on me. Hearing that I was actually taking in and understanding what was going on for him had a huge impact.

GARRY: *Something was changing in me as I recognized the needs behind my use of porn. My belief that there was something wrong with me dissipated, replaced with more self-acceptance. Yet I also felt more vulnerable as long-hidden parts of myself were exposed. When Victoria was willing to wait for me to sort through my process, and not only understood me but even saw something beautiful in how I'd tried to meet my needs, I gained an acceptance of myself that melted a lifelong barrier inside me. When she was able to see beyond my actions to something deeper, more meaningful, I was in turn able to relate to her with a level of intimacy I had never experienced before. It was the kind I had always longed for—without ever realizing it.*

Seeing Garry connect to his needs was a powerful experience for me, and I wanted to explore my own needs: those that were buried in my objections to porn. I was sure that my confusion and anger pointed toward information about myself, so I began the hunt for my own buried treasure.

SORTING OUT MY PAIN

I immediately saw that the idea of examining what we did in our lives to meet needs *sounded* easy, but to actually sit down and inquire within took a lot of effort. I recall thinking, "What is it I'm so upset about? What needs am I attempting to meet when I want Garry to stop looking at porn? How can we be so lovingly connected one moment and then, as soon as this conflict over porn triggers either of us, 'Bam!' we disconnect?" When I tried to answer those questions, I was stymied.

Through NVC I had learned that *feelings* help us connect to our needs. We are likely to have what we usually consider pleasant feelings when our needs *are* met—feelings such as happiness, contentment, and the like—and we usually experience unpleasant feelings—fear, anger and sadness, for example—when our needs are *not* met.

I was definitely feeling fear, anger, and sadness, so logic told me I must have unmet needs. But I seemed to be having more difficulty getting to them than Garry'd had. Finally, it dawned on me that I was trying to figure out needs that related to pain, whereas Garry's had more to do with pleasure. And generally speaking, for me at least, connecting with needs when you're in pain is more difficult.

Also, I had a strong tendency to focus on Garry, not myself. In my mind, our problem was easy: this whole thing was about him. Period! If he were different, we wouldn't have any problems. He was doing something that was harming me and the relationship—and I just wanted him to stop!

While I was struggling with all of this, I remembered from NVC that it's not only feelings that are the gateway to understanding needs—judgments are as well. This was significant because I finally understood that the solution didn't lie in making my judgments go away (which was impossible!) but in using them as a way to figure out what is important to me—in other words, what needs aren't being met for me by someone's actions. For example, when I say someone is a jerk, that judgment tells me that something I value isn't happening for me. Maybe my need for consideration or kindness isn't being met. If I say, "You *should* be more kind," I'm still sitting in judgment. But if I instead acknowledge that the way that person did something didn't meet *my* need, I'm owning that it's my preference to do that thing in a different way, not that the other person necessarily did something wrong.

I decided to examine what Garry was doing that generated so much angst for me and write down all the feelings and judgments I had about it. With pen and paper in hand I retreated to the alcove in the kitchen, a cozy spot in the house I often used for reflection.

Two of his behaviors triggered a lot of pain for me. One was that when we were out in public, at a restaurant or a mall, he often stared at other women. And when I asked him what was going on for him, he admitted he was lost in fantasies about those women. I recalled a particularly painful event.

We were visiting a seaside restaurant with a man Garry had met through a sailing club. All the waitresses wore shorts and tight tops, and Garry stared at them, barely speaking to me or to his new friend. It was a nightmare for me. When we were finally alone and he confirmed for me that, yes, he had been lost in sexual fantasies, I was livid. "What the hell were you doing back there? I think you need help, Garry, when you can't even be present and considerate for one lousy hour. I feel humiliated that my partner is off in fantasy land while I'm sitting right next to him. But, oh no, God forbid that anything take away from your precious fantasy time!"

As I thought back on this event, I still got upset about it, so I thought it might be a good place to investigate. I started with my emotions: what was I feeling when I thought of this event? I was mostly angry and hurt: clear indicators that I had needs that weren't being met.

Next up I wrote down my judgments. "He is so immature! There is something really wrong with an adult male who can't even hold a conversation because he's so lost in fantasy! I feel like I'm with a teenager instead of a grown man!"

Next I went hunting. When I said those things, what did I want? Which of my needs hadn't been met? I thought for a long while, looking over the list of needs to see if anything seemed to fit. *Consideration* was on the list, and when I read it I had a visceral response to it, as if something inside me had jumped to life. I thought about the word *consider* and how yummy it feels when I know I'm being considered. I wrote that need down and continued to look the list over—and came upon *respect*. Again another visceral response. Hmm ... Yes, there was something about this need that applied to the situation, but there seemed to be more to it than that. I sensed I had more judgments, so I turned my attention back to them. I wrote down, "He should be paying attention to me!" I went back to my list to see what need I was looking for in that statement. I came across the need *to matter*, and the answer seemed obvious: I wanted Garry to see me and value me. I wanted to matter to him, and when his mind was elsewhere at the restaurant and not at the table with me, I didn't experience that I did.

I was glad to be able to see what the need was, but I felt no relief from the anger or from the judgment. Agitation returned. Wasn't this supposed to bring relief? Wasn't this exercise supposed to make me feel better? Once I knew the needs behind my pain, wasn't that supposed to fix things?

I shook my head, stood, and began circling the room. There was a missing piece here. Then it came to me: I realized that I was making Garry responsible for *meeting* my needs for consideration, respect, and mattering. Of course I would feel agitated if the only way I could meet a need was through a person who wasn't meeting it! I returned to my chair and tried again, this time only looking at the need *within me* that hadn't been met in that moment. And it came to me with clarity: *I need to matter.* I closed my eyes. I let go of worrying about whether

Garry was doing something he shouldn't, or not doing something he should, let go of wondering whether my need was going to get met, and gave myself permission to simply have that need. Almost immediately, my anger shifted to sadness.

Sitting there with my eyes closed and connected to *I need to matter*, I remembered something from my past: a moment, just a quick memory. *I was trying to get my mother's attention. She was sitting on the couch staring into space, and no matter how I tried she didn't see me, didn't hear me. She was somewhere else in her mind, as she was much of the time. I didn't understand then that she was mentally ill; all I knew was that I was terrified being there alone.*

Suddenly I understood the panic I felt when Garry stared off into a world where I believed I couldn't contact him. It was the same panic I had felt as a little girl. A veil lifted and I could suddenly see what had been hidden behind it all along. Garry's behavior was triggering old pain from long ago—pain I hadn't even remembered until now.

I cried for a long while, tears of relief and tenderness, as I finally allowed myself to feel what it was like to matter to myself. I realized that we all carry with us old pains, and that as a result it can be frightening to look closely at events and emotions in the present. I also realized that even pain we think we have buried has a way of powerfully affecting our present lives.

My relief came when I thought about how I felt inside when I mattered to myself. I felt stronger inside and wondered whether, had I been in touch with this need on that day, I might have done something different, such as excuse myself and go home or speak up.

My tears came to an end, and I took a deep breath. I'd

gained some real insight. But I realized that even though I had connected with what was going on for me when Garry stared at women in public, it still didn't explain why I was so upset about his looking at porn. All I knew was that I was livid when he looked at other women's bodies as I sat in the next room. Yes, I already knew that I wanted that attention he was lavishing on others, but I was pretty sure there was more to it than that.

I hated that his porn of choice was what I would call idealized images of nude women. He told me he never compared my body to theirs, but I didn't believe him. How could he not? And the very things he chose them for—their youth and beauty—were the things that triggered a painful place in me, one where I believed I was loved for what I looked like on the outside, not who I was on the inside. I realized that, yes, some of my judgments were about him—"looking at porn is wrong"—but my first response was to turn the judgments on myself—"I'm not beautiful enough."

I felt that old panic again—pain and emotion from the past—that came from the constant voice that lived in my head: "You're not good enough. You need to be thinner and prettier and …"—whatever it was that I wasn't. It was that voice that had contributed to a bout of bulimia in my twenties, which I had overcome when I made a conscious decision not to believe what society told me about beauty. Now my old fear was resurfacing, and I could see that my belief that I was not good enough had never really gone away; it had just been hibernating.

So when Garry looked at porn, it tapped into a mountain of pain spanning years, stimulating a nauseating mixture of fear, sadness, and rage. I wanted to be seen for who I was. I didn't want to be stuffed into a box that dictated what it meant to be female in this culture. I didn't want to tell myself any longer that I was all about my breast size or that the right kind of underwear would ensure that my man was happy.

I looked over the list of needs again, and a few jumped out at me. I connected with the need for *acceptance* right away. At first I thought what I wanted was for Garry to accept me, but after some thought I saw that what I really wanted was to accept myself—and truly feel that acceptance—regardless of what was happening around me. I wanted to somehow anchor myself in place so I couldn't be blown around by what others did or said. I wanted to trust that I was okay just the way that I was and that I could let go of the endless mind chatter that told me I was supposed to be somehow better than I was.

Slowly, I was able to allow myself to connect with how important *self*-acceptance was to me. I felt into how delicious it was to access that place within myself and let go of trying to get it anywhere outside of me. Somewhere in the midst of this, I also realized that I had a need *to be seen*. Not seen for what might be pleasing to others physically, in a tits-and-ass kind of way, but for what was in my heart.

This was a satisfying piece of the puzzle, but I knew there was more, so I moved on to my judgments about Garry. When he looked at porn I wanted to scream at him: "Wake up! You're wasting your life away looking at this stuff. It isn't going to get you what you really want! You have a living, breathing, live woman here who loves you. Put your attention here in the real world, with us! And another thing: porn is just plain dehumanizing, to you and to others!"

Whew! Just by writing these judgments down, I could feel anger and sadness churning inside. It took real effort to take my attention off Garry and what he wasn't doing right and to look inside myself for my needs, separate and apart from him and his actions. But it was important for me to do just that.

I stared at the needs list for a long time. I was blocked—what in the world were my needs behind these judgments? After a while, something began to come to me. It wasn't exactly on the list, but it was important to me nonetheless: Garry's actions didn't reflect what I valued in the world.

I've listened to enough interviews with ex-porn stars to know that there is a lot of suffering that goes on in the porn world, and I don't want to support that in any way. I just don't see any evidence of porn contributing to the quality of life in a way that I would like to see. I don't see it cultivating compassion or caring or love, values that are very important to me. In fact, I worry that it does the opposite, in that it doesn't allow people to be seen in their fullness, and that it cuts us off from being with ourselves and others in meaningful ways. I recognized that porn was an attempt to meet needs that were important for some people by creating a place to express a variety of desires (meeting the need for authenticity, for example), but I also believed that, overall, it encouraged seeing people as stereotypes (women are only good for sex and men will do *anything* to get it).

As I got in touch with all of this, I was starting to see that maybe underlying my acute discomfort with Garry's behavior was a need for the ease and comfort of being with someone who shared my values.

I sat back in my chair and closed my eyes, taking in

all that I had discovered. My new awareness softened me and helped me see my pain in a whole new light. I had less judgment of myself—I could see that my feelings and judgments were coded messages about my needs and values that I had to interpret. They were pointing me to what was most important to me. Gaining this new understanding was not only important for me; I was pretty sure that if I could convey it to Garry instead of giving him my judgments, I would get a *very* different response.

That was enough for one day. The sun had set and the kitchen alcove had grown dark, so I put my pen and paper down and decided to let what I had discovered percolate.

An Attempt to Meet in Rumi's Field

About a week went by before I told Garry some of what I'd discovered. I had hoped his heart would soften as mine had earlier when he told me his needs. It didn't. I was disappointed by that, and saddened. And it made me wonder whether there was still some blaming energy behind my words or he was reacting to something else entirely. Then he shared what he was experiencing.

GARRY: *For some reason, I couldn't hear Victoria's needs as just that—her needs. Even though I knew intellectually that she was expressing what she valued and what was important to her, I still feared I was responsible for her feelings and for fixing them. What was even worse was that now I believed I was responsible for the plight of millions of women!*

It reminded me of what I had felt sometimes growing up. Since my mom and dad had a strained relationship and my father often wasn't around, my mom turned to me to be the man of the house. I felt responsible for things I didn't even understand. What I really wanted was to just be a kid, to be free and have fun. Now that I think about it, that's all I want to do when I look at porn: to be free and have fun. But now Victoria wanted to connect it with so much more.

I was baffled. I didn't know how to hear what she was saying and acknowledge its validity without taking responsibility for fixing her pain.

Even though this was *so* frustrating for me and didn't fit the vision I had about what would happen when I told him my revelations, I still had hope that there was something to this idea that needs motivated everything we did—and that if we understood those needs, a shift could occur. Just the fact that he could describe what he thought might be at work in him gave me hope that I could get the connection I was longing for.

It was clear to both of us that this new approach to life and relationship was difficult and would take time. It has been challenging for many reasons, not least because we've both been steeped in a culture that supports fast answers and quick results. There were times when I wanted the quick fix that came with the "there is a right way and a wrong way of thinking" paradigm. This path we had chosen was asking for a shift from the only way we had previously known to relate to each other, and such a deep shift takes time and patience.

So if you're thinking, "Oh, get real. There's no way my partner and I could have these kinds of conversations," rest assured, Garry and I aren't always able to do it either. Even today there are times when our pain intervenes and we can't even catch a glimpse of Rumi's field. At such times, we can still feel isolated and angry, and we sometimes shut down.

But we practice; and then we practice some more. And when we get a sense that we're in over our heads, we try to remember to slow down, take small steps, and be patient with ourselves and each other. We've found that we rarely resolve things in the heat of the moment. Sometimes we just give each other some space and wait until we're both more receptive. We've learned that though we may be afraid and want to avoid the subject at hand, if we open up to the fear and face it in small steps, it's not so scary after all. And having faced our fears, we find greater peace within ourselves and an ever-stronger connection with each other.

We are still unfolding.

chapter 6:
The Shame Game

Even though Garry and I were now talking more about porn and what was really going on for each of us, I noticed I was afraid to open up about it with anyone else. I desperately wanted to, but inevitably every time I thought about mentioning it I ran into an immense wall of shame. I felt too vulnerable to expose what was going on in my life, even with my closest friends; in fact, because they were so important to me, it was their judgment I feared most of all. What if they thought Garry was a pervert? What if they thought staying with him meant something must be wrong with me? What if …? What if …? At the time, it seemed as though I was the only person I knew suffering with this problem—this despite the statistics I'd found that offered overwhelming evidence I couldn't possibly be alone.

I didn't only feel shame when I imagined talking about porn; I felt it at other times as well. For example, if I walked into a room and found Garry looking at images of young, naked women on the internet, I became overwhelmed with shame. What Garry was doing was certainly the stimulus for the feeling, but how I responded was all about me and my old pain—not about him, the women, or what he was doing. On came all the old voices telling me how awful my body must seem to him after looking at such idealized bodies. This self-loathing often lasted for hours, and while I stewed, I tried to think of ways to make myself thinner or prettier.

When I was embroiled in what I can only call a "shame attack," all I could do was ride it out until it subsided. Once it did, I could try to identify what was going on during those times. Looking back, I can see that there were layers to my shame. Sometimes there were just two or three layers, while at other times they seemed to stack up as high as the Eiffel Tower. The bottom layer of shame was what I told myself about what I didn't look like. "You're getting older, Victoria. Your skin isn't as smooth as it used to be." Then I added another layer of shame: what I should look like. "Maybe I should get a face lift" or "If only I could fit into those old jeans," and on and on. On top of those layers, I felt ashamed that I was even thinking like that and believed that if I had greater self-esteem, none of this would be happening. Somehow I had come to believe that men only loved confident, secure women—and when I felt this way, I was neither. I was terrified I would lose Garry's love if I spoke about these awful feelings and thoughts.

REDEFINING SHAME

I looked up the word shame in the dictionary. The definition read: "a painful emotion caused by having done something wrong or improper." This didn't resonate with me—I knew that many people feel shame when they aren't doing and haven't done anything wrong. Something else had to be going on, and I decided to write my own definition:

> *Shame is a story I tell myself that I am not okay the way I am.*

When, in response to Garry's looking at porn, I tell myself I am not pretty, wanted, or sexy enough, I'm saying I'm not okay the way I am. And this destructive story provokes fear, sadness, and anger—and shame.

I wanted to talk with Garry about my struggle with shame. I believed that he must be feeling his own share of it as well, so I asked him if he would be willing to explore the emotion with me. I wanted to see just what kinds of messages he and I had about porn. I had the sense that, if we could identify the stories—about why it was shameful, about what our thoughts about porn itself were—we could move forward more easily. What judgments did he have about viewing porn? What stories did I believe about him, about porn, and about myself? And how were our stories contributing to our feelings of shame?

GARRY: *At first this seemed really hard to do, I think because I believed my stories so thoroughly that I couldn't fathom that they were something I might be making up about myself. It was also difficult to think of anything specific. I knew I felt shame about porn, but at first I couldn't say why. After a while I was able to identify a thought: "There must be something wrong with me to want to look at bodies and sex over and over again. I must be some kind of pervert." I also had a vague sense of being worthless. "If this is what my life consists of, then it's pretty pathetic."*

I think there is a stereotype that a guy who looks at porn is a nerd who can't function in real relationships, so he hides out in fantasy. A part of me believed that about myself.

There was a time in my life when I really believed I was worthless and I had lots of shame about it. I owned a business that wasn't doing well, and my nine-year marriage was coming to an end. I felt ashamed of my inability to succeed at either of these; in fact, I believed I was a total failure. These feelings were overwhelming at times. I couldn't escape the voice inside my head that repeatedly told me what a failure I was.

My shop didn't get much traffic, so I hung out in the back looking at porn on the internet, and while I was lost in that world the voice subsided and I felt some relief. When I stopped looking, I felt numb for a while, which was better by far than the feeling I had when I told myself I was a failure.

But those recriminating thoughts of failure inevitably resurfaced; and when they did they were even worse than they had been before. I think this was because I also felt shame about looking at porn, so in a sense I was piling more shame onto my already full plate. But what did it matter? I was already thinking I was worthless and feeling hopeless. Without understanding what was happening, I created a painful cycle of looking at porn to relieve the feelings of failure and shame, feeling worse after stopping and then looking at porn again to make the painful feelings go away. Some part of me knew that my escape into porn was temporary and illusory and that the habit was only reinforcing my pain, but I didn't understand what was happening, and I had no awareness of other possibilities for handling my feelings. I was simply looking for some relief from the painful feelings that came from my belief that I was worthless and a failure.

As Garry shared his stories with me, once again I felt compassion; I could see even more of his pain and vulnerability. It was clear to me that the stories he believed about himself were the source of his suffering. Yes, his marriage and his business had been falling apart, but what did that mean? That he was a bad person? A failure? A pervert? No, those are merely labels. Perhaps it was just time for his relationship and business to come to an end. Yet these were the messages he told himself again and again. Was there something wrong with him because he liked to look at sex? Maybe not—perhaps it was simply an attempt to find some kind of beauty or connection in his unhappy situation.

I thought of a quote from a man named Huang Po, an influential Chinese master of Chan Buddhism. "The foolish reject what they see, not what they think; the wise reject what they think, not what they see." If Garry had been able to heed this wise man's words and reject his self-deprecating thoughts, he would have rejected the stories about something being wrong with him and his actions. What would be left, then, would be pure, observable facts: his business wasn't making as much money as he would have liked, and he had less joy in his marriage than he had hoped for. Period.

After listening to Garry's stories of shame, I shared with him something from my past that was still affecting my life. I asked him to hold me while I told him the story.

"I was fourteen years old and just coming into my sexuality, and since my family didn't talk about sex, my girlfriends and I were on our own. We hung out with the local boys and explored kissing, getting touched, and touching. It was so exciting to think that these guys liked me. For once, I didn't think I was invisible, and I was getting the attention I had longed for. This went on for a while until one night, it happened. We were kissing and he was feeling me up and pretty soon things took a different turn. I remember feeling on the one hand so confused and scared about what was happening, but on the other, curious."

Garry just held me with a steady presence. I'm not sure why I was so afraid to tell him this story. I guess I felt exposed—I was showing him something I had kept locked away because I still felt shame around it. I continued.

"Then it happened pretty fast. We were on the ground in the backyard, and we had sex. It was over almost before it began, and instead of feeling as though I had just experienced something spectacular, I was left with disappointment and a looming feeling that I had just done something I would regret."

I took a deep breath, and Garry gave my shoulders a gentle squeeze.

"The worst part of it all was that word got around that this boy and I did it, and suddenly I had a reputation as a bad girl. Overnight, it seemed as though I was hurled into a world of good and bad, and I was on the wrong side. After that, it seemed like I got more attention from boys, but some of my girlfriends pulled away. Though I acted as if everything was fine, I had devastating thoughts of being flawed, worthless, and unlovable. I bought into the whole good girl/bad girl dichotomy, and from that time forward I worked at building a façade of being a good girl ... but deep down I believed that I was and always would be a bad girl."

Garry still held me, and I noticed my breathing was shallow as I waited for his response. In some ways, it seems ludicrous that I would even think for a moment that he would respond in any way but a loving one, but I guess the part of me that still lived in hiding was afraid to be seen. Recognizing that part, I began to grieve: for all the years I'd carried around feelings of worthlessness and for how much I berated myself, and mostly because I could now see that the thing I feared most—being the bad girl—was a creation of my own mind. I had unconsciously believed this illusory story from that moment forward.

Garry wrapped his arms around me tighter now, and I leaned into him more as I cried. When at last I stopped, it occurred to me that we both might have needs buried somewhere in our shame. In NVC, when we experience what I call the "unpleasant emotions," such as anger, fear, and sadness, it points to needs that are not being met. It seemed like every road led to needs in some way, and I was beginning to see the pattern.

I looked back and saw that my needs as a fourteen-year-old girl were all about acceptance: acceptance for who I was, sexual urges and all. And now, all these years later, I still had that need. I wanted to be able to let go of the stories that told me I wasn't okay, and I wanted to know in my very being, through and through, that I was valued.

This struck a chord with Garry.

GARRY: *When I thought about all the harmful things I told myself about what it meant that I liked to look at porn, I was amazed I could even function. If I said those same things to someone else, I would be put in jail for harassment! So why did I do this to myself? When I looked at the needs that weren't met when I berated myself like that, I thought, as did Victoria, that I needed acceptance and value. I wanted to be able to acknowledge that this was what I enjoyed doing without equating it with something being wrong with me. I wanted to live my life knowing I had value.*

Once Garry and I consciously recognized these stories—held them up before us in the clear light of day—we realized that we had a choice: we could continue to believe in them or we could instead illuminate the needs we were trying to meet and acknowledge that there could be other ways to meet them. For us, the choice was clear.

OPENING UP TO OTHERS

Now that I was able to more clearly see how much I hid in fear of judgment, I wanted to face it. The more I faced

it, the more I gained courage, and the more courage I
felt, the more I was able to be vocal about the subject
of porn. Shortly after Garry and I opened up to one another, an opportunity came my way to bring this part of
my life out into the world at an NVC workshop. I had
been with the group for several days and felt as accepted as I had ever felt anywhere. Also, considering that I
might never see these people again, I felt some measure
of safety "coming out" in this setting. I waited until the
last session of the day was almost over and then raised a
trembling hand. Marshall Rosenberg called on me.

My heart raced in my chest as I told the group what I
was struggling with: that my fiancé, whom I loved very
much, was viewing porn and that we were struggling
with how to deal with this in our relationship. To my
huge relief, I wasn't met with the judgment I had feared.
Instead, Marshall welcomed the topic and, during the
few minutes remaining, suggested possible needs that
some men may be meeting when they look at porn.

But the real gift came when the session was over.

Many people approached me wanting to talk more
about the issue of pornography. Women shared stories
about their partners' viewing habits and how they handled it. Some men spoke about looking at porn, and they
were grateful I had brought it up because it was something they had been dealing with as well. On that single
evening I met eight people who were confronting the
same issue. Some of them were struggling, while others
had found peace with it in one way or another; and all
were grateful that I had raised the subject.

By this time, I already understood that pornography
was far more prevalent in society than I'd realized, and I
knew that everyone had an opinion about it. But what I

hadn't grasped until that moment was the sheer number of people who were dealing with the very same issue I was: Someone I love looks at porn. How do I deal with it? Do I stay or go? How do I make sense of it all?

Was this particular workshop a freakish hotbed of pornography? That was hard to believe. Or was this problem truly as widespread as it seemed, simmering under the surface in homes throughout the country? Either way, I no longer felt alone. I had faced my shame and moved through it. As I lay in bed that night reviewing the day and evening, I felt a warmth flow through my body and a glow in my heart; my need for connection and acceptance had been met.

That day at the workshop changed the course of my life. When I was met with acceptance and understanding instead of judgment and condemnation by others—for both myself and Garry—I was able to break through the wall that kept me from opening up. I understood that shame is not inherently part of the issue of pornography; instead, it comes from the stories we tell ourselves about it. This knowledge was a powerful new tool, and Garry and I had found yet another way to understand one another and ourselves better. This would prove to be invaluable on the journey we had chosen.

We also knew, without a doubt and from that moment forward, that we were not alone.

And neither are you.

chapter 7:
Sleeping with the Enemy

The pendulum swung. One day we were connecting and deepening our understanding of one another and the next we were in conflict. Even though we were experiencing new—and oh so satisfying—ways of relating to each other, our old habitual patterns drew us back toward conflict again and again. They were strong.

> *"I don't get it. Why is it such a big deal that I look at porn? It's not like I'm running around chasing women. Why can't I have the freedom to do as I please? I'm not hurting anyone!"*
>
> *"'Not hurting anyone'! Oh I guess I don't count, is that it?! And how about that you spend hours every day dehumanizing women by looking at them as objects, only valued for their tits and ass?!"*
>
> *"They like it! They wouldn't be doing it if they didn't want to. You're just upset because you have a negative self-image."*
>
> *"Oh my God, how naive are you? Lots of women do this because they're told from the day they were*

*born that they're only valued for their bodies—why
wouldn't they do things to try to be valued?"*

"Says you!"

*"You know what? Just forget it. I don't even un-
derstand what I'm doing with a moron like you!"*

*"Fine. If that's the way you feel, then what are
you doing here? See, this is one of the big reasons I
like porn so much. I don't have to put up with this
kind of crap when I'm with those women!"*

*"Well, guess what—you can have them. I'm
outta here!"*

One slams the door, angry and ashamed. The other feels
desperate, alone, and hopeless.

Sound familiar?

Sometimes our home was more like a war zone than a
refuge. As soon as either of us felt upset, we stopped
looking at each other with love and instead saw each
other as the enemy. We each wanted to make the other
wrong, thinking that if we blamed and pointed fingers
at each other we'd feel better.

We were both fighting for something very important.
For me it was liberation, for myself and other women,
from the confines of our conditioning. I saw porn as yet
further evidence of how for so long we have been objec-
tified, reduced to two-dimensional creatures that exist
to be whistled at, commented about, and judged. And it
wasn't just women, either; men, too, were stereotyped in
porn. My cry was for more humanity. Garry was part of
the oppression—I was sleeping with the enemy!

Garry wanted liberation, too, in a sense: liberation from the shackles of what he had been told he could and could not do all his life. He had already lived with so many constrictions, so many limitations, that he heard my desire for him to stop looking at porn as one more person telling him what to do: he was sleeping with the enemy!

We both continued to think that if only the other would see the error of his or her ways, everything would be okay. We each fought hard for our way to be seen as the right way and to show the other how he or she was wrong. It didn't work; our fights only left us weary and bruised. Not only was the whole process unsatisfactory, but we found it was doing serious damage to our relationship. Each time we fought with this right/wrong energy and tried to make the other responsible for our pain, we undermined the very foundation of our relationship, disempowering both ourselves and each other.

What Is an Enemy Image?

The term *enemy image* is not new; I didn't create it. Though the first time I heard it was at an NVC workshop Marshall Rosenberg was facilitating, it has been around for a long time and has, in fact, been the focus of many studies on the psychology of war. In order for people to kill without feeling the reality of what they are doing, they must be able to label others—individuals and groups, nationalities and religions—in ways that dehumanize them. These labels allow a person to disassociate from other human beings and view them as something less than human, which makes violence without remorse much more likely. This is how atrocities such as slavery, the Holocaust, and genocide can happen.

Although such examples are extreme, and perhaps seem like they can't possibly apply to daily life, the phenomenon is pervasive and is frequently carried out in day-to-day relationships. As soon as we think we have been wronged in some way by our partner ("I can't believe what a *jerk* I married—he can't even remember my birthday!") or the guy who cuts in front of us in line ("What an *inconsiderate ass!*"), we place our attention on their foibles and nothing else. In those moments, we believe we know the right way to behave and the other person is wrong, without understanding what might be behind their actions. And who knows why they act as they do?

We attribute certain characteristics to other people when we feel the sting of our angry response to our own unmet needs. In that instant, "the other" becomes an enemy and responsible for—the cause of—our pain. Even though the everyday behaviors I've just described seem minor compared with the earlier examples of the enemy image, the phenomenon itself is not minor: label and dehumanize; make the other an enemy.

ANOTHER POSSIBILITY

At an NVC International Intensive Training session I attended, Marshall Rosenberg talked about how these enemy images severely limit our capacity to compassionately connect with others. He explained that if we can understand the needs someone is trying to meet through their actions, we can step out of judgment and into understanding. Like the peace activist Gene Knudsen Hoffman, who said, "An enemy is one whose story I have not heard," Marshall pointed us to another possibility: put the focus on connecting with the needs behind the person's actions and see how that can shift the energy of the exchange. Instead of going down the same old dead-end road of the right/wrong paradigm, choose a different path.

At first, I reacted to this idea with fear and judgment: *"What is he, crazy? Some things are just plain wrong, and doing this connecting crap ain't gonna change that! Slavery was just plain wrong. The atrocities at Auschwitz were just plain wrong. The Native American and Rwandan genocides were just plain wrong. Isn't it our job to speak out against these evildoers and stop them from doing these things, teach them and others why they're so wrong? Does Marshall think all I need to do is understand what's behind these kinds of actions and it will be all right?! If that's the case, then I guess it's okay that the porn industry is making fifty-seven billion dollars annually worldwide by fusing our sexuality to objectification. It's okay that it's an industry that is so totally inconsistent with the values that our nation is supposed to hold dear: equality, justice, and mutual respect!"*

Such was my mental tirade that I couldn't continue to listen to the discussion. I left and went for a walk. I had spent many years caring passionately about issues like women's rights, racism, gay rights, and environmental degradation. How would it be possible for me to connect with the people I saw as the enemy? In my mind it didn't seem conceivable that I could be authentically myself and connect with the enemy at the same time.

I didn't want to be one of those people who seemed to exhibit the saccharine version of compassion, the kind that stems from the thought "A good person is compassionate, so I'll act that way whether I really feel it or not." For me, this version oozes sincerity on the outside, but it's empty on the inside. I was considering bagging the whole workshop and going home when a thought from deep in my mind made its way forward and held my attention. Suddenly I was aware that I regularly did the same thing my enemies did. I said the same things about them that they said about women, people of color, gays, Muslims, etc. Things like how terrible they were and that there must be something wrong with them. We were on opposite sides of the same viewpoint!

I stayed for the rest of the workshop, deciding to at least make room for this idea: that I and those others were not so much enemies as people looking at the same things from different points of view. On my drive home I had lots of time to think, and I asked myself some vital questions: Why would I want to see those who cause pain as anything *other* than the enemy? What's in it for me? And even if I want to, how in the world do I tell someone what's really painful for me without seeing their behavior as wrong and telling them so? Isn't that impossible? Don't people *need* to be told when they're doing something wrong?

I reflected on how much I have longed to live in a world where all people are seen as valuable, and kindness replaces violence ... and how odd it was that I found myself engaged in violent thoughts as a means to bring about peace. I recalled a quote by author Audre Lorde: "The master's tools will never dismantle the master's house." Could I have unknowingly been using the tools that generated enemies while all the while longing for peace? Suddenly my world no longer made sense. Now I was uncomfortable with my old way of thinking about enemies—and at the same time, very uncomfortable with this new paradigm. My mind was in chaos.

I tried to remember if I had ever had an experience outside this so-called enemy image paradigm. I couldn't think of anything in my own life, but I did recall a shift happening in my heart as a grueling event had unfolded in an Amish community not long before. They'd had more than just cause to go down that path of enemy images, yet didn't.

On October 2, 2006, Charles Carl Roberts IV, a thirty-two-year-old milk truck driver, took a number of hostages in a one-room Amish school house. He eventually killed five girls, ages seven to thirteen, before turning the gun on himself. It is difficult to comprehend the kind of pain their families and friends experienced in this situation, let alone the ripple effects that could influence generations to come.

What moved me most about that terrible event was the extraordinary way in which the Amish community handled it. They were able to feel their pain and mourn their loved ones without taking it out on the family of the murderer. In fact, the entire community was concerned for the well-being of his family, and many people sent notes of condolence and forgiveness. After the girls were laid to rest, many people from the Amish community attended the funeral of Charles Carl Roberts IV: the man who had forever changed their lives.

At the time, as those television images spilled into my living room, I couldn't fathom this kind of response. These people had every justification to be enraged, even vengeful. *So why weren't they?* Until then, I had believed that this kind of forgiveness, the ability to hold pain while staying connected to another, was the province of only the most special of people: Christ, Buddha, Gandhi.

REALIZATIONS

Still driving and contemplating this extraordinary event, I basked again in the love I felt whenever I thought of what this Amish community had modeled for me, and a new awareness bubbled up from my unconscious. Something about this story helped me see the obstacles I had to understanding what Marshall was talking about. And I suddenly found myself crazy with excitement! The things I grasped in that moment were threefold.

My first understanding was that until now, I hadn't had a clue about how to be aware of the love that always underlies the face of difficult feelings. The image that came to me was that love was like the sky, always there. Until then I had believed that when a cloud of feelings obscures it, love is gone. I had somehow come to believe that love naturally comes and goes, as any feeling does, instead of perceiving it as a force that never waivers. What a very different reality I could be living if I could understand this! Was it possible that when I was angry—or even enraged—I could approach any situation from a foundation of love? That love, like the sky, would always be there regardless of the anger?

My second realization was of a long-held belief: if I understood a person's needs it meant I condoned his or her actions. As long as I had the equation (connecting with needs = condoning), I was always going to create enemy images. But maybe if I could separate the needs from the actions, I would have a better chance of stepping outside this old way of relating; after all, it wasn't getting me what I really wanted. I don't believe for a moment that the Amish condoned the behavior of the man who murdered their children, but they were still able to stay connected to his humanity.

Third, it struck me that I had already been practicing connecting to the needs behind behavior I didn't like! Even though I was thinking I had no idea what this new kind of connection might look like, I had actually done this before when I heard Garry's needs. Just that recognition now gave me hope that what had at first seemed impossible, was possible.

MAKING CONNECTIONS

My drive home had turned into a journey toward the kind of compassion the Amish community had exhibited. And I wondered if it could be available to all of us.

As I headed back to the man I loved and yet sometimes saw as my enemy, I actually felt excited. I knew that my life with Garry and what we were dealing with formed the perfect environment in which to put this new idea into practice—a place where the change in my enemy image paradigm could come to fruition.

I shared with Garry all the details of the workshop, with an emphasis on the idea of enemy images. He was intrigued. I asked him if he wanted to share any enemy images he held of me.

"Tell me again what an enemy image would look like," he said.

"It's any way in which you see me as the cause of your pain, and, when you see me in this light, as someone you want to change or punish in some way."

Almost before I finished, he said, "Yeah, I sure do have an enemy image of you!" I guess I was hoping for a little more hesitation on his part, but I was also happy we had something to work on. He jumped right in.

"I see you as someone who keeps me from doing what I want by disapproving of me—there are certain things I can't do because you won't like them. It connects to the same pattern I've been in my whole life, one of people telling me what I can and cannot do, and what I should be like according to their ideals: still more restrictions and constrictions in my life. I hate feeling like this. I want to be able to do as I please according to *my own* values."

I had mixed feelings about what I was hearing. I wanted to pull back when I heard him say that I kept him from doing things and that I was disapproving. But I quickly realized that in response to what he was saying, I was actually doing the same thing to myself that Garry was—creating an enemy image of myself by thinking that now *I* must be somehow bad or wrong. Then I noticed yet another part of me that was making an enemy of him, thinking, "It's not my fault! Take responsibility for your own life, you jerk!"

Now that I had awareness of this phenomenon, I was beginning to see how pervasive it was in my life. When I saw him as a jerk I lost touch with his humanity, and when I then turned my violent thoughts on myself I couldn't see my own. I could see that both of my responses were judgments that kept me from seeing the basic needs we were both trying to meet.

Then I noticed I had yet another response to Garry's words: compassion for what he was feeling. I knew very well what it was like to have judgments in my head and blame others for my being restricted, judged, and unheard. Whether I was *actually* blaming or criticizing him or it was only happening in his image of me, it was still upsetting for him.

I remembered my desire to see if Marshall's ideas held any truth, so, for the moment anyway, I decided to put all my thoughts aside and just stay connected to Garry and listen. I played back to him what I guessed was happening for him.

"Are you frustrated because you really want to experience freedom," I asked him, "to experience being the one fully in charge of your life?"

"Yes," he answered immediately. "It seems that all my life I've had to be careful about what I did because of how it might upset others. I honestly don't think my mother cared a whole lot about me personally, but she constantly told me what I had to do so she wouldn't look bad to others. She seemed more concerned with what the neighbors might think than what was going on for me. I had to be the model son so she could feel good about herself."

"Are you pissed because you want to be cared about as you are—you want acceptance?"

"Yes! I just want to be me, not what someone else wants me to be."

I felt my tension begin to dissipate, and I could tell

that I was starting to break through my enemy image of him as I grasped the needs behind his seeing me as disapproving and limiting him. I felt a flurry of excitement.

Then I asked Garry if, when I expressed my distress about porn, he heard it as disapproval of him and his actions.

He paused for a moment, then said, "Actually, I'm having an amazing insight. I'm realizing that the voice that tells me others are disapproving is really my own voice. It's like I've internalized it and I project it onto everyone. It doesn't matter if they really aren't judging me—I still hear it that way. I believe they're saying disapproving things, but in reality, it's me saying them."

"Wow, Garry! It's amazing to me that you're able to see that. And I'm really excited now, because I think that if you get that, it's likelier you will be able to hear me clearly—instead of hearing me through your own disapproving voices."

"I think when you reflected my needs back to me," Garry went on, "something became clear. It's as if a wall has been preventing me from seeing my pattern of making others the source of disapproval—I've wanted to make this about everyone else. I've spent a lot of time concealing parts of myself and cutting myself off from others so I can avoid their judgments. Something about exploring this with you has helped me see that this is something I carry with me wherever I go."

I sat there mesmerized and amazed by what he was saying, and I experienced us connecting on a whole different level. Marshall Rosenberg had said that our connection to the feelings and needs of others changes the dynamics of the interaction, and our consciousness shifts as well. This had happened to me on my drive home. I had seen that I didn't have to agree with Garry to hear him. I had seen that *connecting to needs* didn't equal *approving the behavior*—and now I was actually experiencing it. I was beginning to understand that I could disagree with what someone did or said and still *not* see him as an enemy. And that wasn't the only gift here. There was something in this new connection that opened us up to more possibilities for change than my former defensive or critical stance ever had.

My turn came when Garry asked if I saw him as the enemy. I didn't need much time, either, to come up with my enemy images.

"I have two that kind of dovetail together. First I feel really angry and sad when I think about this big porn industry that values money over people."

"What do you mean?" Garry asked.

"Well, I believe that the porn industry is basically in the business of selling bodies and sex for profit at the cost of others about whom they don't give a hoot. They turn people into body parts. We don't see who these people are in any real sense, which cuts us off from their humanity. Did you know that sixty-five to eighty-five percent of the people starring in these films have been sexually abused as children? And that many of them are drug addicted as well? I saw an interview with two men who scout out women for the films. They go into bars to find women who are either already addicted to drugs or who are susceptible to them. I don't want to support any industry that doesn't reflect the kind of caring for others that I believe is important. When I see you sitting in front of your computer, participating in something that might be taking advantage of people who need help and support, not sex work, I believe you're not only giving your seal of approval but actually perpetuating their suffering."

Garry's eyes were getting that look, and I knew he wasn't connecting to what I was saying. "What in the world does this have to do with me looking at porn? I'm not doing any of those things!" he said.

"I know you're not directly, but by supporting it with your viewing of it, you're saying that it's okay to see people as objects, as things for entertainment, without any regard for their well-being. You're saying that it's okay for people to be treated in the ways that they are."

Garry looked both perplexed and frustrated, and I suddenly wanted to shut down. I had that familiar hopeless feeling I'd had much of my life when I tried to communicate something that seemed really clear to me but that no one else understood. I didn't know where to go next. I found myself feeling angry at Marshall Rosenberg, whom I didn't even know personally, because Garry and I couldn't figure this out. Now *Marshall* was the enemy! I wanted to believe him, but it was clear that trying to connect to those I see as my enemy was getting me nowhere.

Then I realized I was basing my connection with Garry on the condition that he connect with me in the same way. What if I tried to understand where he was coming from and then waited to see where we went from there? This ran counter to all my conditioning, which told me to hold him as the enemy in my mind and make him wrong; this was, after all, a new thing I was trying.

"Garry, are you frustrated because you'd like some understanding about how I could connect the whole porn industry with what you're doing?"

"That's only part of it," he said. "From my perspective, looking at women as sexual stimuli is considered normal, so it's really difficult for me to make the leap from looking at porn to the abuse of women. And anyway, honestly, that argument isn't a powerful motivator for me to want to change because I can't connect to allegations about some big industry in the same way I can connect to you. So when you tell me how my looking at porn impacts you, that's more important and immediate to me and a much more powerful motivator. I don't want to say that those other things aren't important and real, but it's difficult for me to relate to them directly ... I can, though, see how it affects you."

For a few minutes I was confused. I thought I already *had* told him an important way porn impacted my life, and I wanted to be heard about that. For me, porn was related to an entire system that was at the core of my pain, and I wasn't sure I could separate them. On the other hand, he was clearly telling me what would work better for him, so I made an attempt to bring it closer to home. I tried the best I could to take us out of the game of right/wrong and back to my unmet needs.

"I feel sad and angry when I think about how much conditioning I've taken on about what it means to be female in this culture," I said. "I've learned that my value, my worth, is all about what I look like and has little to do with who I am. There are times when I haven't a clue how to love myself, and that realization is frightening. When you look at porn, I wonder if you value me for myself. Now it's getting clearer for me ... I want to be valued for who I am. I have this thought that you value *ideas* of women or the *fantasy* of women, and I'm worried that will have an impact on our relationship and how you see me—some impact we're not even aware of at the moment. I wonder if we'll grow closer and more real with each other, or if we'll drift apart because the reality doesn't hold up in the face of all that fantasy."

I had been sitting stiffly in the chair as I spoke. When I finished, I relaxed and asked, "Can you relate to that better?"

Garry's expression had changed from looking hardened and confused to soft and open.

"Yeah. I think I'm starting to get a sense of what's going on for you now. You have enemy images of me because you want to be valued just the way you are and you want my actions to support that. Is that right?"

As he spoke, my entire being eased. "Thank you for hearing that," I said. I paused, thinking; there was something else emerging from my consciousness. "I definitely would enjoy your support, and I have no doubt about that. But right now I'm noticing that I would also like to hold on to my own value no matter what you're doing or what the porn industry is doing."

"This sounds like it has something to do with your need for personal power, or self-responsibility. Am I going in the right direction with that guess?" he asked.

"Yes, that's it. I want to take responsibility myself for the quality of my life. This brings me back to what I was trying to get to earlier when I talked about the porn industry and my belief that you support it. I place a high value on taking personal responsibility for the choices I make in my life, and I also like it when others do the same."

Garry seemed more open to what I was saying this time. "Okay, I think I can relate to that. There is something about the care of all people that's very important to you. And there are parts of the porn industry that don't meet your needs for care or justice."

"Yes! You're definitely getting it now."

"When you want people to take responsibility for their actions, it sounds like you just want people to be aware of how their choices impact the lives of others. Is that right?"

It felt *so* good to hear that he understood what was important to me! "Yes, that's it, Garry. Thank you for seeing that."

Our enemy images, and the pain of separation that came with them, were melting away. Our ability to see each other fully, to touch our humanness by seeing what was in our own and each other's hearts, was ascending. From this miraculous place, I could see myself and Garry very differently from the way I did when I was locked in my thoughts that he was wrong and needed to change.

It was at that moment that I recognized the essence of what Marshall was talking about. He wasn't asking me to give up what I believed in or give in to anything I was uncomfortable with; he was pointing me to a different place, one in which I could create change. He was asking for a prerequisite for change: *connection,* not only to my own humanity but to that of others as well. It was with this connection that change could come from love, not fear; from understanding, not violence. This was that powerful place I had reserved for the Gandhis and Buddhas of the world, and now I knew that it *was* possible for all of us to dwell there. Garry and I didn't yet have the years of practice that would build trust and confidence over time, but I now had enough experience of it to know that what we'd just shared would change me forever.

chapter 8:
Acceptance

I liked where we were headed: the struggle between us now looked like a doorway into a greater understanding of ourselves and each other. Still, there was a persistent hum of tension running in the background of my life stemming from the fact that I was living with a guy who looked at porn. I wanted relief from that tension, but I wanted to stay with him as well. I also wanted to be fair to Garry and give him the space to figure out his own life. I didn't want to send mixed messages by telling him I loved him one minute and then punishing him for his desire to look at porn the next. Nor did I want to live in denial about my feelings—I certainly didn't want to feel as though my decision to stay meant that the issue was closed, done, a thing of the past. I wanted room in the relationship to bring up anything at any given moment.

In essence, I wanted to be able to accept Garry for who he was, yet also reserve the right to be upset about porn if I felt that way—and those two states of being seemed contradictory. If I accepted him, didn't that mean I accepted all of him? Didn't that in turn mean I couldn't express any confusion or anger I might have?

There was something about acceptance that seemed to trigger discomfort for me, and I wanted to come up with a clear understanding of the word. The whole concept was challenging, and I quickly became confused, so one day I explored my concerns by writing down the flurry of questions bouncing around in my mind:

If I accept something, does that mean I don't care about it anymore?

If I still feel pain, does that mean I haven't really accepted it?

How can I change something if I accept it?

Are acceptance and indifference the same thing?

Is tolerance different from acceptance?

I also grappled with this:

Is acceptance a way of justifying something I don't agree with?

Seeing my questions in black and white helped me understand more clearly what was behind my fear and confusion. I realized that, in my head, *acceptance* was connected to and defined by *agreement*. I believed that if I accepted something, I was agreeing with it—basically, approving of it. And once something is approved of, it's unlikely to be discussed: after all, what's the point of discussing something that's been settled?

Ultimately, I feared that if I accepted Garry's looking at porn, I was essentially telling him I wouldn't feel distressed about it ever again—and as a result, we would never need to discuss it again. As I looked at this more closely, I saw that behind my fear was the desire to have personal power over what came into my environment, and I believed that if I accepted things as they were, I would lose that control.

GARRY: *I, too, had uncomfortable feelings and confusion about this word acceptance. I feared that if I accepted Victoria's pain, somehow I would be responsible for it, or that her pain would never change. I didn't want us living in some kind of la-la land where it's all good and there's nothing to be upset about. I wanted room for us each to be ourselves — not some stilted arrangement based on avoiding painful topics. I wanted to welcome whatever came into our lives.*

ACCEPTANCE VS. NONACCEPTANCE

It was challenging for me to believe I could have both acceptance and pain at the same time; in my mind I could only have one or the other. The answer to this dilemma eluded me for quite a while, and Garry and I discussed it frequently at home, in the car, on walks. It wasn't until I questioned my beliefs about acceptance that I began to see a way through the confusion.

I remembered two events from my past when I had already experienced having acceptance and pain at the same time. The first had taken place after I broke up with my first love. The pain seemed unbearable, and I fought against it with my whole being until I seemed to be frozen in time; I couldn't go back, yet I couldn't move forward. Then one day as I was taking a shower, sobbing uncontrollably, a subtle but clear voice—my own—told me very calmly, "It's over. Accept it." A huge wave of relief passed through me, and I knew without a doubt that I would at last be able to move on. I still felt hurt, but my acceptance of the reality of the situation mellowed that feeling, transforming it into the sweet, pure pain of loss: much different from the pain that comes from resisting what is true.

The second was a recurring experience. I recalled how, in my practice as an acupuncturist, I had seen people approach their illnesses in different ways. Some people resisted the very fact of their illness, seeing it as a burden they'd been unfairly saddled with. They spent most of their time and energy wishing things were different—wasting valuable energy they could have used for healing. Others, although they felt pain and sadness about their illnesses, accepted what was happening, so they didn't expend energy railing against their predicament or wondering, "Why me?" But here was the key: accepting reality didn't mean they sat back and said, "Oh well, I'm sick, that's the way it is, and I'm not going to do anything about it." That's apathy, not acceptance. Instead, rather than asking, "Why me," they asked, "Given that I am ill, how can I move forward?"

I realized after recalling these experiences that acceptance wasn't about giving up or giving in or trying to transcend what I was feeling; it was, simply, accepting what was true. An image of nonacceptance came to mind: there is something I dislike sitting next to me, and I either deny that I'm upset about it or try to transcend it by pretending it isn't there. Both responses mean I'm resisting reality. In contrast, if I accept reality, I could allow myself to sit next to this thing and be curious about its existence; I could even wonder what it had to offer me. And I recognized something else: if I couldn't bring myself to sit next to it with acceptance, then I could at least become aware of my resistance and accept that.

I carried this image into my relationship with Garry and realized that, if I couldn't accept that Garry was going to look at porn, I could sit next to my anger or sadness and accept that. This was very different from my approach in the past: in my nonacceptance, I had turned my back and tried to make Garry's looking at porn go away.

Putting Acceptance into Action

Working this out in my head was one thing, but putting it into practice was another. Then I learned why: I was grappling with the idea of acceptance on a conceptual level, but acceptance is a human need, and our needs are qualities of energy that are alive in us at all times. Not concepts at all, but real states of being that we live in.

I was learning to understand needs at a whole new level, in that the things we value (needs) aren't just words with a particular meaning; there is also an emotional component to them that we can feel in our bodies. I wondered then: What if I could access the feeling of acceptance within me and *live* it instead of trying to figure it out in my head? Hmmm ... Could I *be* acceptance instead of *do* acceptance?

This new notion—that there was already an amazing feeling aspect of my values within my physical body, that it had its own energy and all I had to do was to connect with it—held tremendous appeal for me. So I found a place to sit quietly and connect with this energy. As a way to evoke the emotional aliveness and the physical sensations connected to acceptance, I relived how I had felt when I accepted the loss of my first love. Then I just sat with that experience in my body. Immediately, my body relaxed. I could feel myself letting go of tension, and there was what I would call *flow* to my energy as my desire to resist, to push against something, diminished. From that physical, embodied experience of acceptance, life looked very different. And I knew that feelings of resistance, either to myself or Garry, would give me a way to tell that I wasn't in touch with this flowing energy of acceptance.

There was more. Acceptance felt light, expansive, open. I smiled when I felt it. But it also had depth because I was seeing and respecting life as it was.

I tried imagining accepting Garry as he was, porn and all. Immediately, my body flinched, and I found myself feeling fearful, thinking, *"No!"* I took a deep breath and faced this fear, sat down beside it, and waited. I knew it had something to tell me. It didn't take long before I realized that the feeling was, once again, all about needs. I was afraid that *my* needs wouldn't be met if I accepted Garry's looking at porn. When I realized this, I relaxed, because I knew I had a way forward: what if *I* made sure to keep my needs present, no matter what? Could I, then, with that commitment to myself, love Garry just as he was? I took it as a yes when the fear within me lifted.

I went back to the thought of accepting Garry as he was. I imagined him sitting next to me surfing the web for images of sex or nude bodies. As I stayed connected to my desire to accept him as he was, watching him at the same time, my resistance fell away. In that moment I saw how tiring it was for me to have nonacceptance in my life, to keep pushing all the time against something that loomed so large.

I also felt incredible love for Garry as I realized, again, that he was simply trying to meet his needs in the best way he knew how. Suddenly, I became acutely aware that my constant desire to change him had been sending the message that he was not okay, that he was wrong. I also saw how it prevented me from being present with him: when I viewed him through my lens of resistance, I kept him at arm's length.

What a wonderful new view of things! I felt sad knowing I had spent so much time pushing against life, but I was excited to be experiencing the living energy of acceptance.

Garry noticed the shift in the energy of our home.

GARRY: *When I started to actually feel Victoria's acceptance of me as I was, it was a powerful experience. I felt so loved, and it was as if, through her eyes, I was able to catch a glimpse of my own humanity and value. And I could tell she wasn't just pretending; it was genuine love and acceptance of who I was.*

Once I started getting how good this acceptance stuff felt for me, I naturally wanted to be able to give her the same gift in return. I began looking at the ways in which I didn't accept Victoria. I saw that there were parts of her, like her feelings of jealousy, that I didn't want to accept. I interpreted her jealous feelings as her way of saying I was untrustworthy.

Whenever she felt jealous, I thought there was something wrong with me. Or if she felt fear or anger for any reason, I became afraid and didn't want her to have those emotions. I would start to scramble if she was upset because I believed I had to fix her distress so that I could be okay again. Instead of examining this in myself, I got angry with her for putting me in that position. It was a little scary when I saw just how deeply ingrained this pattern was: it kept coming up again and again.

When I thought of accepting Victoria the way she was, I couldn't do it, so I had to start with myself and see if I could accept my own resistance. What if I was trying to meet needs by resisting? What could those needs be? This seemed like an easier place to start. Once I looked closely, I saw that when my reaction to her being upset was to think something was wrong with me, my need was to feel okay. The only way to feel okay in that circumstance was to make her wrong, to believe there was something wrong with her instead. I began to see that this was a weird way to try to meet my need for self-acceptance — to make her wrong so I could be okay.

Once I saw how important self-acceptance was to me, I also saw how my attempts at self-preservation were coming at a cost to both of us because of the way I had to see her when I did this. I wanted to find a way to accept us both at the same time. Recognizing this, I really began to change and let her have her feelings without beating myself up.

Garry came to me one day and told me about how challenging it was for him to be accepting when I was feeling jealous.

"I've noticed lately just how much my belief that I'm responsible for your feelings is getting in the way of my being able to accept you as you are," he said. "I'm sad about that. When you get jealous about the women I look at when we're out in public, I can't be there for you because I'm caught up in thinking, either I must be a schmuck or there's something wrong with you. I really don't like thinking either one. And lately I've been able to see that when I can't be there for you, I'm actually trying to accept myself."

I was elated to hear his new awareness about something I was still sensitive about. I had felt him disconnect from me many times, and I had longed for him to be able to reach out to me when I was feeling jealous and just be there for me—maybe even pull me to him and whisper in my ear how much he loves me, that I have nothing to worry about and that I'm the love of his life. Instead, he usually got mad at me, and in turn, I got mad at him. Both of us wound up with bruised hearts.

"I love hearing that, Garry, because I now have some hope that the painful dynamic that's been going on between us might change."

"Yeah, I'm hopeful," Garry said, "but still a little wary because I see that this idea that I'm responsible for your feelings is pretty ingrained. It seems like it's impossible to change sometimes." Then he added, "But, yeah, I am more aware of it than I have ever been before, so that's good news as far as I'm concerned. I guess I get scared when I tell you these things I've discovered because you'll expect me to change overnight or something, and I just don't think that's possible."

I thought about this for a moment. "Are you saying you'd like acceptance for where you are at this point, and that you don't want to feel pressure about getting it right or having to change overnight?"

He nodded.

"So maybe what we're both accepting here is that we have this dynamic sometimes, and that we'll work it out."

"Yes! That really says it all for me right there," Garry said. When you decided to stay, what made me happy wasn't that everything was perfect and settled; it was that you accepted what we were dealing with and stayed anyway. Acceptance, to me, is a fundamental trust in each other to work it out."

"Mmm … I like that!"

An Invitation to Show Up as We Are

I was grateful for that conversation and for Garry's growing awareness about that particular dynamic between us. There are, most definitely, still times when we both feel hurt and we can't connect to our own need for acceptance, and that's okay—we just accept *that*. Acceptance is finding what we can accept and being with the things we can't until we find a way to shift. What carries us through those rocky times is the trust that both of us are doing the best we can.

We started living in acceptance more of the time, and it shifted how we related to each other. I believe that many of us have a core idea that there is something fundamentally *wrong* with us, with our circumstances, or with both. It is deep-seated and painful. It plays out over and over again in the background of life, shaping our relationships to everything and everyone. This new acceptance in our lives was like a balm for that deep wound, and it changed our relationship to ourselves and those around us.

Practicing acceptance was a beautiful invitation to show up as we were, in our lives and with each other. We were creating an environment where it was safe to show each other our inner selves. We discovered that there is something magical about being seen and loved exactly as you are, and for who you are.

GARRY: *It was clear that our desire to change one another was dwindling. We noticed that our anger and fear still got triggered, but it didn't go as deep or last as long. We were moving through things much more easily.*

It was around this time that I noticed a difference in my desire to look at porn. It was already losing its appeal, but I was now looking at it much less than before. I saw that some of my wanting to look at porn was me just wanting to rebel and prove that I could do as I pleased. Without her resistance to push against, I lost the urgency to rebel.

Now that she had stopped resisting and judging, I stopped blaming her and started questioning what I was doing with my life, and why. I found myself wanting to be more like the man I thought she wanted me to be. A fundamental trust was developing, and it was safe to reveal myself more and more.

I realized that Garry and I were onto something profound. We were creating a relationship, day by day, that at its core had principles of love that took each of us fully into account. Something inside me felt like it was aligning with the cosmos, like I was now living in better accord with the way life was meant to be experienced.

Who would have thought that struggling with porn could lead to enlightenment? As Rumi wrote, "Be grateful for whatever comes because each has been sent as a guide from beyond."

chapter 9:
Deepening Our
Relationship to Needs

Something amazing was happening in our lives. Garry was losing interest in porn, and of course I was excited about that. And for my part, I was changing and growing in the ways I related to him, to myself, and to the people around me. But there was something else happening, something even more profound: we were entering into another level of awareness.

It seemed that we were moving from a pain consciousness (relating to one another only through our discomfort and distress, and seeing each other as either right or wrong), into a needs-based consciousness, one in which we related through mutual understanding of the values that motivated our behaviors. This was Rumi's field, and we were spending more and more time there.

We found that simply understanding the needs behind our actions didn't mean that we no longer had our ups and downs. But it did mean that we were able to see any situation we were in more clearly, and if it wasn't working for us, we could begin to do something about it.

When we had been locked into right-and-wrong think-ing, there was only one option: fight for (our own) *right* position. When we instead worked to understand the needs motivating our behaviors, we were able to ask ourselves some important questions and attain some very welcome and refreshing clarity.

We asked ourselves questions like these: If we start with the premise that looking at porn is a strategy to meet needs, once we identify those needs, are there oth-er ways in which Garry can meet them? And for either of us, when we choose a particular strategy to meet a need, does our choice sometimes neglect other needs? If so, what should we do with that information?

GARRY: *I wasn't forcing myself to change in any way; I basically just started to lose interest in looking at porn. When I thought about why that was, I realized that it had to do with feeling safe enough to open up and figure out what I was really after. Once I was able to see a need I was trying to meet by look-ing at porn, I realized that there were other ways I could meet it.*

Until now, I hadn't understood what I was after; I just figured that it was something in porn itself, so I kept going to it over and over again. For example, I noticed that I especially liked to look at porn after work. I didn't realize—not until I really thought about what I needed during that particular time— that it was because I felt deadened after a day of work, and looking at porn filled me with sensation and helped me feel more alive. Once I understood that, I began to find other things could give me that feeling as well.

I was reconnecting with myself more and finding the life inside me. Now that I felt pretty safe in this relationship with Victoria, talking with her about what was going on for me was a new way to meet that same need to feel alive. Or sometimes I could meet it by getting out and taking in the beauty of the place where we lived, or by making sure that I got out sailing more often. Those things and others like them filled up the space that porn used to fill, and they fulfilled my need to feel energized after a long day at work.

It was freeing for me to realize this distinction: the difference between a) needs and b) the strategies to meet them. For instance, Garry *wanting more aliveness* (need) is different from Garry *wanting to look at porn* (strategy) *to get that aliveness.* He had a lot of choices about the ways in which he could feel alive. Porn was just one of them.

And the same was true for me. I realized how attached I had been—and in many ways still was—to the *ways* I met my needs; now I was learning how much variety I had to choose from, and suddenly my world filled with possibilities. I noticed that I had made Garry my sole strategy for meeting many of my needs, especially my need for connection, when we moved to California. Getting clear about what I was after helped me branch out in other directions.

I also saw that I was never in conflict with the *needs* Garry was trying to meet by looking at porn. I *wanted* him to feel that spark of life; I just wished he would choose other ways to accomplish that—sailing, maybe, or getting a job that didn't make him feel dead inside by the end of the day. Hearing him make this distinction for himself gave me hope that we would be able to find strategies that could work for both of us.

SOME STRATEGIES WORK BETTER THAN OTHERS

Another distinction we were making was that some strategies were more effective at meeting needs than others, and more beneficial to us. Our need for companionship, for example, might be met by going to a bar filled with people, but if we hated loud places, we would be better off looking for other ways to find companionship.

After we got to the bottom of a particular need we were seeking to meet—which, as I've noted before, is often not an easy task—we could then ask ourselves if the way we were going about meeting it was *both* meeting the need *and* fulfilling us, or if instead it met the need but offered no real satisfaction or fulfillment. I had often wondered why I kept returning to the same behavior again and again even when, ultimately, it was never very satisfying. In exploring this critical distinction between needs and strategies, I started to get why that was. When I used one of my old, unsatisfying strategies, my need might be met temporarily, but ultimately, I wasn't satisfied. Despite that, I would keep going back to it because I didn't understand what I was really after. I think it was the American writer Eric Hoffer who said, "You can never have enough of what you don't really want."

Here's an example of what I'm talking about. I had a longstanding pattern of pleasing others because I wanted to be valued (my need). Pleasing others did indeed meet that need—albeit temporarily—but it didn't really fulfill it in a deep, satisfying way. In this equation, my feeling of being valued depended on whether another person decided to value me or not. Still, I kept trying to please others over and over again, because doing so gave me a *taste* of what I was looking for. Ultimately, with the benefit of learning the distinction between my needs and the strategies I used to meet them, I realized that the fruits of this repeated behavior didn't last, and that the results weren't as fulfilling as I wanted them to be. Through this journey that Garry and I were on, I came to see that connecting with my own value was a much more stable, fulfilling strategy.

GARRY: *I saw that I wanted intimacy, but that the kind I was getting with porn had its limitations. After all, the women I was looking at didn't talk to me. I had had many experiences of intimacy with women in my life, but I always held so much back out of fear of being vulnerable that I never quite connected. I was afraid I would be rejected if I let them see the parts I kept hidden.*

Once I truly felt acceptance from Victoria, I began to feel safe enough to let her see the parts I was afraid of — the monster I feared I was. This was the key to true intimacy for me. I was now sharing myself, all of myself, with another human being, and that was satisfying in a way I could never have imagined before. Finding this level of intimacy was like finally tasting an orange that had only been described to me before. With Victoria, I had a two-way street, something I didn't get from porn. There was something really magical about feeling fully accepted by another human being.

Another eye-opener was when I realized that I looked at porn to meet my need for freedom. For most of my life I had gotten messages that I shouldn't look at porn. This pissed me off and I wanted to rebel. I wanted choice and the freedom to do as I pleased. But when I looked more closely to see if looking at porn was really satisfying that need in me, I had to admit that no, it wasn't.

There were times when I felt frustrated about my desire to look at porn so often and for so long. This wasn't freedom. With true freedom, one can look or not look, and either is okay. But I felt compelled to look, and it became just a kind of prison. Because of this compulsion, I didn't have the autonomy and choice I wanted. When I thought about what it would be like to really experience being in control of my life, I realized that was true power, and that I would rather have that than what I had been experiencing with porn.

Discovering our needs was like finding a magnifying glass that could help us see the details of our lives; and knowing the details gave us much more choice about how we lived. We were no longer stuck figuring out whether something we did was good or bad, right or wrong. Instead, we could ask ourselves what we were after and whether the strategy we had chosen was working as a way to meet that need. It was wonderfully freeing.

Meeting Needs Here, Not There

Another differentiation that helped us make decisions about our lives was the realization that sometimes the choices we made to meet one set of needs meant that other needs might go unmet; meeting a need *here* could mean not meeting one *there*. If I go on vacation because I'm after fun, for example, that choice may not meet my need for ease when it comes time to pay the bills.

GARRY: *This was true for me as well. I often looked at women in my workplace and thought of them only in reference to how appealing they were to me. This was fun for me, but there were times when I was sad about it. Once I investigated why that might be, I saw that judging women by how attractive they were got in the way of making a genuine professional connection with them and giving them the respect they deserved.*

I also noticed that spending so much time looking at porn, meeting one set of needs, meant that meaning and purpose in my life got shoved to the wayside. I wanted to accomplish more than that, and I wondered what I was doing with my life. At the end of it, looking back, was I going to be happy that I had spent years sitting in front of a computer screen looking at sex? I wasn't sure, but I had my doubts.

Looking at life through the lens of needs was both clarifying and satisfying. We found ourselves more willing to tackle difficult issues we had been reluctant to face in the past because so often they had seemed to lead down dead-end roads.

PUTTING THE DISTINCTIONS INTO ACTION

One of the issues I hadn't really dealt with yet was that I was still uncomfortable going out in public with Garry, with his looking at other women while I was at his side. The strategy I was using to deal with it was to stay at home—pretty limiting. I knew this wasn't going to help me face the situation in the long run, so I began to look at what I was doing from a needs perspective. What need was I meeting by not going out with Garry? Well, it was damn uncomfortable for me to go out with him, and I didn't want to feel that way, so I figured the need was for ease and comfort. Once I could name what I was after, I saw that while staying in gave me some relief, it was only on the surface, and it was temporary. The issue didn't go away just because I stayed in. Until I came to terms with it, I knew I wouldn't have the deeper relief I was really looking for.

When I looked at what I was doing, I also saw that I had other needs that weren't being met when I stayed home. First, I wasn't free. I was letting my fears hold me captive. I wanted to be able to go out any time and not worry whether it was going to be a hellish experience. Also, I didn't have the range of choices I wanted. I wanted to be able to choose to stay or go, but locked in my fear, I was limited to a single choice—staying. I also wanted to understand what was going on inside my reactions to being with Garry in public. It always seemed

like it was out of proportion to what was actually happening in the moment. I sensed that it was connected to
something much bigger, and I wanted to see what that
was.

Now that I could acknowledge that this strategy
of not going out with Garry wasn't as life-serving as I
wanted, I reevaluated it. What other strategies could
I use to meet my needs for ease and comfort as well
as freedom? Garry agreed to help me explore my options—reluctantly; he knew the subject was charged
with emotion. But he also knew that we had to do something other than rattle around the house for the rest of
our lives. He was right about the emotions: just knowing
what we were about to discuss was painful for me. But I
took a deep breath and started the conversation.

"Garry, I'm very uncomfortable when we go out in
public and you stare at other women. When I've asked
you what's going on when you do that, and you tell me
that you're fantasizing about them, I get really pissed
off. I hate knowing that you're with me and thinking of
someone else. One of the ways I meet my need for love
is through connection and presence, and when that suddenly disappears around other women, I think that you
don't love me—and also that I don't matter to you."

"So are you saying you want to know you are loved,
and that you matter to me?" Garry asked.

"Yes, that's right," I replied. "But there's more. It taps
into a well of pain that seems to be tied to my experience
with my mother's mental illness and how I couldn't get
the connection I wanted with her. When we go out and
your attention is focused on other women, suddenly that
same feeling sweeps through me—as if I don't exist. And
I panic."

He took this in. "Do you think the need behind that is something like … you want to be seen?"

"Yes, that's true. But also, I want to know I matter. Plus, when you stare at other women when I'm with you, I don't feel loved or valued." I took a good look at Garry to see how he was reacting, and I realized he looked sad. I asked him about it.

Garry said, "I *am* sad that something I do has such an impact on your happiness. But, it's like with the porn—I don't want to just tell myself I'm bad for doing what I'm doing and just stop for that reason. I want to understand it."

"I do too," I said eagerly. "I very much want to know what's going on for you. It would really help me to understand if you could tell me the needs you think you meet when you stare at women like that."

Garry took a few minutes to gather his thoughts, then began. "I'm not sure. This behavior is so ingrained in me and I've been doing it for so long that I wonder if it's just a habit."

"It must be meeting some need—otherwise you probably wouldn't keep doing it."

"I guess that when I look at another woman when we're out, I'm wondering what it would be like to get to know her and what it would be like to be with her. It brings back the feeling of being in a new relationship, when everything is new and exciting. I feel best at the beginning of a relationship, because that's when a woman accepts me and I accept her. As time goes on, though, I hide parts of myself that I think she doesn't want to see. And then I become resentful and … I guess deadened somehow, and I start looking for things that will help me feel alive again. By and large, I do that by looking at and fantasizing about other women. And then the cycle repeats."

God, I hated hearing this. Did Garry feel our relationship was coming to an end? Was he hiding things from me? Was he feeling deadened inside even now? "Now I'm worried that this cycle is playing itself out with us," I said, "that you're keeping parts of yourself hidden."

Garry smiled. "Not at all. In fact, I find that I'm not looking at women in the same way anymore. Honestly, I don't think I will ever not look at an attractive woman and appreciate her beauty, but I'm not getting lost in the fantasy anymore. Just being able to talk about all of this with you, and knowing you can hear about this part of me without telling me to get rid of it or else—it's great!"

"So back to your needs," I said, excited now at the chance to delve deeper into the reasons for this change in him. "It sounds like you want to feel alive in yourself, and you want acceptance for *all* the parts of yourself so you don't have to hide the ones you think are unacceptable anymore. Is that it?"

"Exactly. That's it."

I loved hearing his needs because they helped me get out of the stories I told myself about why he did what he did—stories like "I don't matter to him" or "he doesn't love me."

Then Garry said, "I think we should start going out together so you can see where I am now, not what you remember from before. And I want to be present to you. You're precious to me, and I don't want to miss out on what we can enjoy together outside our home. How about we try it? And if we're out and my old pattern happens again, then we'll look at the needs it brings up and use them as a way to reconnect with one another."

I liked that idea. I had been staying in to meet my needs for ease and comfort. Now I was beginning to believe that I just might be able to go out and feel at ease too. I could see now that behind Garry's actions were his needs for acceptance and aliveness, and I had more hope that I might not be so inclined to take it personally. If we went out and things got uncomfortable, I felt confident we would be able to talk about what we were experiencing in the moment instead of battling about who was right and who was wrong.

And so we went out. We drove to one of our favorite restaurants in a picturesque town up the road. I was tense, afraid of feeling pain once again, but also hopeful and excited. As fate would have it, we were seated at a table in the corner across from an attractive woman eating by herself. The gods were wasting no time on us!

In such a situation in the past, both of us would have retreated to our internal worlds, not speaking about our emotions or desires or fears. This time was different. Instead, we huddled together in our corner and told each other what we were thinking and feeling. I asked Garry if he was drawn to this woman.

"Yes," he replied. "I think she's attractive and I'm curious about her."

My stomach pitched—I hated hearing that! He brought his attention back to me and took my hand and squeezed it. "I am also very much here with you, and I'd like to know what's going on for you right now."

"I'm feeling a little panicky, but I'm also glad that we're able to sit here and talk about it—you know, instead of falling back into our old patterns, either going into silence or arguing about it. I also really, really like that you pulled me closer to you. There is something about that that puts me at ease. I guess I feel your presence, and that meets my needs for love and care."

We were revealing ourselves to each other: that worked on me like a healing balm these days. The honesty between us helped me see exactly what we were dealing with in any situation we faced, and that put me at ease.

Throughout the meal we went back and forth like that, each of us sharing what was going on for us. Garry was behaving differently from the way he had in the past; he wasn't so lost in fantasy, and he was with me in a way that met my need for presence by actually sharing his experience with me. And I freely shared what was going on for me. We made room for it all.

We had managed to create a life-enhancing interaction instead of the destructive one we had previously found ourselves trapped in over and over again. When I was able to hear Garry's needs, it helped me connect with him; he felt that connection and brought himself forth, and he was able to experience that sense of aliveness he had been looking for. He was energized by greater presence with me, which met my needs—to be loved and to matter. And as a bonus, we both felt more at ease.

I was so excited by what was happening, I wanted the whole world to know! I thought about what it would be like if we all could look underneath our behaviors and see what the underlying needs were: what a different world we could live in. I thought of the man behind the curtain in *The Wizard of Oz*. When we lift the curtain and reveal our needs, we get to see the real person behind the actions.

On that day, the truth of what we had found on our

journey together rang suddenly clear. Garry and I were leaving behind a way of relating and communicating that we had been caught up in our entire lives, and we were connecting on a whole new plane—one that was much more loving, caring, and respectful. I loved this guy, and he loved me, and now we had a way of communicating that reflected that.

A Decision to Stop Looking at Porn

Garry: *It was around this time that I decided to stop looking at porn. My desire to look hadn't gone away completely, but it had diminished greatly, and understanding the needs I was trying to meet gave me more choice about how to meet them. Plus I understood Victoria's needs more clearly now. I loved her, and the thought that my actions stimulated pain for her was something I no longer wanted to continue, so I told Victoria that I was ready to stop.*

Wow! I couldn't believe my ears at first. "What did you say?!" It was music to my ears, and I wanted to hear it again.

"I've decided to stop looking at porn altogether. Now that I have a clear understanding of the needs behind it, I want to focus my time and energy on finding other ways to get them met. I also really care about you and how this impacts you, and I want my actions to reflect my love."

"Are you sure you can you give it up completely?"

"Yes, I'm sure. I may still feel the urge sometimes—

the desire hasn't completely disappeared. But at least now I'm confident I can be open with you and talk to you about it when it comes up."

My heart melted into a big puddle of love hearing him say that. I was happy ... for a while.

But I still had a vague yet persistent anxiety, and at first I couldn't figure it out. How could this be? After all, I had gotten the very thing I had longed for. I pondered this for quite some time until it became clear to me what was going on.

Even though numerous times in the past I had taken my focus off Garry, instead turning inward to see where my feelings were coming from, I had always unconsciously gone back to looking outside myself for answers: it was such a deeply ingrained habit. But now that he had stopped looking at porn, I no longer had his behavior to focus on—and I was all alone with feelings of anxiety that I thought would have lifted when *he* changed his behavior.

It was time to reconnect to myself to see what gifts my unexpected discomfort might have in store.

chapter 10:
The Guest House

The Guest House

This being human is a guest house.
Every morning a new arrival.

A joy, a depression, a meanness,
some momentary awareness comes
as an unexpected visitor.

Welcome and entertain them all!
Even if they're a crowd of sorrows,
who violently sweep your house
empty of its furniture,
still, treat each guest honorably.
He may be clearing you out
for some new delight.

The dark thought, the shame, the malice,
meet them at the door laughing,
and invite them in.

Be grateful for whoever comes,
because each has been sent
as a guide from beyond.

I chose to repeat the poem from the beginning of the book here to give you another opportunity to contemplate it, as I believe it so eloquently gets to the heart of how Garry and I had been able to continually deepen and transform our relationship. And it was a godsend when the time came for me to confront another painful emotional pattern of my own.

Years ago when I first read it, it evoked an intense longing for something I found difficult to articulate. Something about the way I had come to view life was causing me much suffering. I believed there was something wrong with me and, generally speaking, that there was something wrong with any uncomfortable feelings or thoughts I might have. I believed that in order to be happy and safe, I had to push away the bad things I found in myself and others. This poem flew in the face of that belief. It told me that everything in life has something beautiful to offer and that I don't have to push any of it away. In fact, it told me that there is treasure waiting to be found even in the most challenging feelings, if I would only invite them in gratefully and truly see them for what they are and what they have to offer.

It had been years since I first read the poem, and at last my longing was being fulfilled. I was actually living the poem more frequently now, and so was Garry. We heard our guests knocking at the door, and instead of running for cover we were answering it, throwing it open wide, and saying, "Hello! Come in. What do you have to show us today?"

When porn first arrived on our doorstep, I firmly believed it had come for Garry, not me, and that we needed to figure out how to fix *him* so that I would want to stay with him. But now that he had stopped looking at porn, I could see that I had been mistaken: porn had come to visit both of us.

All those painful places within me, the ones that porn had always seemed to trigger, still wanted my attention even after my home was free of porn. Those uncomfortable feelings had remained behind to ask me what was important and help me discover the answers. I began to see that many of my beliefs and much of my suffering had been with me long before Garry arrived. His actions had stimulated so much pain because they were like a stick probing old wounds.

In the past I hadn't been able to understand that the distress and anguish I felt in my life sought expression, so I closed the door and shouted at them to go away. It was the best I could do with the tools I had at the time. But once I began to see something beautiful in every expression of life, I felt more confident that I could open myself to whatever arrived. And of course, the more confident I became, the more life opened to me.

Jealousy Came Calling

As you know, life doesn't always knock politely. One day I heard it pounding, its heavy fist rattling the hinges. I answered with trepidation ... and there was jealousy on the threshold in all its glory, the jealousy that had been with me for as long as I could remember and present in every relationship I'd ever had. It was still relentless, and I attempted many things to evade it: monitoring Garry's behavior, avoiding the presence of attractive women while I was with him, and even throwing away lingerie catalogs so he wouldn't see them.

I had been deeply ashamed of this green-eyed monster, and I believed I was a horrible person for being jealous. Or I tried to palm it off onto others, making them responsible for it: "You're making me jealous! If you hadn't done what you just did I wouldn't be feeling it!"

My new attitude toward this persistent house guest helped me realize that the jealous part of me was asking to be seen. It wanted liberation—and at last I had the courage to face it and what it had to teach me. But I had identified jealousy as being part of me for so long, something that plagued me and that I wanted to be rid of, that I wasn't sure I had the ability to see it clearly. I decided to ask for help. At first I turned to Garry—without success.

GARRY: *I wasn't up to working on Victoria's jealousy. I had experienced a lot of pain and frustration about it, and I thought that I wasn't the best person to see it clearly either. I knew that my looking at porn and other women had been a big trigger for her, and even though we'd been finding new ways to deal with it, I could easily go back to a pattern of defending myself and blaming her. Knowing this was such a sensitive area, I didn't want to risk it.*

When I told Victoria I didn't want to help her work this through, she was okay with it. I loved that! For much of my life I'd feared that if I didn't do what somebody wanted me to do, I would incur their wrath. I didn't usually get that from Victoria, and this supported me in speaking my truth more and more often.

THE GIFT IS IN THE LONGING

I appreciated Garry's honesty when he told me he didn't want to try to help me in this way because it built trust that he was being honest with me about other things in our relationship. And it allowed me to move on and find someone else for support. Robert Gonzales, whom I've mentioned earlier, was one person I knew I could turn to for help. He had a unique way of showing me how to get to a deeper understanding of myself, and he helped me access my needs so that I could *live* from them instead of constantly trying to get other people to meet them for me. I contacted him by phone, took a deep breath, and asked for help. Robert began by asking, "What is it that you long for when you're feeling jealous?"

What a great question. It immediately led me to look for something of *value* in my discomfort, instead of rushing to get rid of it. Answering the question wasn't easy for me, though. What *was* it that I was longing for when

I felt jealous—what did I need? I ran through the list of possibilities, as I was becoming more and more accustomed to doing, and I noted some needs that might be involved felt more *right* or *alive* than others. I watched for the feeling I had when the right need fell into place like a puzzle piece. After trying several pieces, I finally found those that fit—and the picture became clear and whole.

I realized that, both in general and in my relationships, I wanted to know that I was safe, that I could trust that I was loved. I wanted to be able to let go into something that held me like a net, something sure, safe, and predictable. I wanted to know that I mattered, and that I was important enough to be considered in every situation. Wow! As I leaned into what I wanted, my longing increased. There they were, all the needs I was trying to fill every time I got jealous. Each time before, I had missed what I wanted because I was too busy hating and fearing the jealousy itself—and pushing it away.

It was like flipping a switch, making that connection between my jealousy and my desires for trust, security, and to know that I mattered. I no longer viewed the feeling with disgust. Almost the moment I realized what my jealousy was showing me, I lost the urge to push it away; instead, I felt compassion for myself. I flashed back to when I was a child, and I saw that all my life I had been longing for this feeling of trust and the sense that I mattered. I began to cry as I realized that the same jealousy I had been pushing away so harshly all my life—that I had been so ashamed of and felt such animosity for— had simply been calling me toward my own needs all along.

I also felt sad as I realized how much of my life had

become a search for the right person—someone outside of myself—who could give me these qualities I valued. I had tried in vain to make the people in my circle responsible for making my world safe. And I wondered what it would be like to look to myself for what I wanted instead. A wave of excitement ran through me. It wasn't that I thought I would no longer have to meet any of my needs from the outside—that I would suddenly become the lone ranger, going through life wanting nothing from others—or that Garry's behavior would no longer matter to me. On the contrary, my excitement was more about understanding that I had the ability to take care of myself. And if I couldn't meet my needs for safety and trust in our relationship, my world wouldn't fall apart because I would still be able to meet them within myself.

Touching the Needs Within

With Robert's help, I worked on getting in touch with what these particular needs felt like inside me. What were the physical and emotional dimensions of trust and security? What did it feel like when I was in touch with my need to matter?

I closed my eyes and connected with how *trust* lived within me, the actual sensation of it. When I felt it, my body relaxed and let go. I no longer had to defend myself when I was in touch with trust. I was more malleable, flexible, and relaxed. Playfulness bubbled up—my energy was no longer wrapped up in fear, and I didn't have to push against life. I experienced this intimate connection to trust in my whole body, and I felt confi-dent I could handle life and I would be okay.

When I got in touch with *security*, I experienced be-ing held by something, by a presence. Again, I relaxed and let go as I felt this presence wrap around me, inside and out, letting me know that all was safe.

When I connected to my *need to matter*, I straightened, and I felt a strengthening sensation in my body: I was taller and more alert. I felt something inside my own body looking out for my well-being.

When I was firmly self-connected in this way, I felt more profoundly present. I was more in touch with the life in every situation.

Our conversation went on for about an hour, and by the time Robert and I stopped talking, I was vitally in touch with my needs and immediately sensed a shift in my relationship to myself and the world around me. I was clearer and more alive, and life had a spacious quality. This had an immediate impact on my relationship with Garry.

GARRY: *I noticed a change in Victoria right away. She lost much of the wariness and vigilance she'd had, and I felt easier around her. When she told me the needs she was trying to meet when she was jealous, it allowed me to see what she was really after in-stead of the focus being on the action — mine — that triggered her pain. When she could tell me just how much she wanted a sense of security and to know that she mattered, I wanted to support her in that, and I could do so without the pressure of being responsible for her life.*

The connection between her childhood and how she was with me and in the world had me feeling compassion for her. It had been unnerving, never knowing where her sadness and anger were really coming from and always being on guard for what might trigger them. Knowing which needs came up for her when she was jealous made it a known entity that could be seen for what it was.

In the weeks following my conversation with Robert, a sense of vulnerability lingered. I could really relate to what Garry had meant when he'd told me how he sometimes felt—like a turtle without a shell. I had worn my jealousy like a shell that protected me from the idea that I was fragile, and from my fear that in an instant, someone I love might die—or fall in love with someone else.

Now things were different. That old way of thinking and being began to fall away as I explored my needs instead of the jealousy into which they manifest, and looked within for the source of my own infinite worthiness. I trusted that I was connected to something far greater and more mysterious than I could possibly imagine, and I opened my heart and mind to whatever might come knocking next.

chapter 11:
In the Bedroom

*S*o *what are your fantasies?"*

"*I'm scared to tell you!"*

"*Come on. I'll tell you mine if you tell me yours."*

"*Okay, but you have to promise you won't make fun of me."*

"*I promise."*

Both Garry and I had conflicting feelings about sex and our own sexuality, a result of the many mixed messages we received growing up. On the one hand, sex was everywhere; it was in our faces every day in magazines, on television, in movies: seemingly the one thing everyone desires. Yet other sources—religious traditions and family taboos, for example—warned us it was dangerous, bad, or shameful.

These conflicted beliefs had made it difficult at times to talk openly about our fantasies, and sex had been one more place in our lives where we tended to hide out from one another. But now that we had chosen to walk a path of transparency—being honest with ourselves and each other—we could see this conflict more clearly. And the more obvious it became, the more we wanted to be free from it.

We started by tracing our "good/bad" notions back to our childhoods.

GARRY: *There were lots of mixed messages about desire as I grew up. I was told in so many ways that sex and desire were bad, yet as a teen, I had a ton of desire pulsing through me. Unfortunately, I decided that there must be something wrong with me for feeling it. It didn't feel safe talking to anyone about it, so I just lived with this struggle inside me.*

And it played itself out in my life. When I looked at porn, I was saying yes to desire. For the time during which I immersed myself in it, I gave that energy permission to exist; it felt liberating to be able to go wherever my desire led me. I enjoyed those times when desire had the reins, but as soon as I finished, all the messages I believed about how bad it was came flooding back. "There must be something wrong with me" and "I'm so pathetic" frequently entered my mind when I thought about how much time I spent reading about or looking at sex.

My challenge with desire and my beliefs were very different from Garry's. I grew up believing that women were both devalued and valued. We got paid less, we weren't as visible in places of power, we were told we should be nurses, not doctors, and the role of caretaking children was downplayed. On the other hand, we certainly were valued—as *objects of desire.* So I learned that my own power lay in attracting men, whose power was acknowledged in the society in which I lived. I sought to figure out what men wanted from me so I could give it to them as a way of having a sense of my own value. This way of relating stemmed from a belief that I wasn't enough the way I was, that I was lacking. I tried to obtain my worth from men, those who I believed could give it to me.

That's how my motivation to look outside myself for my identity and value began, and it encouraged dependency. The more I sought value outside myself, the more disconnected I became from myself, and this in turn fed the cycle of looking for validation from others, believing they held the key to my happiness. Surprisingly, I was still able to have friendships with girls and eventually women, but often, lurking around in the complexities of our relationships were competition and comparisons.

I came to believe that if I wanted to be loved, I had two options. I could be a good girl or a bad girl. My young mind decided I could be one of the bad girls by having sex, and be desired, but in the end I would be valued less. If I chose the good girl side, I had to suppress my sexual feelings. I balanced on this sexual tightrope, and I feared that if I misstepped I would have no identity at all—so I chose a bit of each reality. I kept my sexual feelings in check, but I also tried to remain sexual enough to be an object of desire.

Longing for More Self-Connection

Years passed and I began to wonder who the heck I was. I had been so busy being what I thought everyone else wanted me to be that I no longer had a clue about what made me tick. I longed to have an intimate relationship with myself, something I had never had and wasn't even sure was possible, so in my mid-twenties I came up with a plan. It put me into free fall.

Although I wasn't conscious of it at the time, I chose a strategy that emulated a ritual nuns had been performing for centuries. I cut off my long hair in favor of a crew cut. I wore only comfortable, nondescript, functional clothing. I decided not to be in a relationship until I could find my connection with self. I chose not to get on a scale and to eat whatever my body wanted, not what I thought I *should* eat to stay thin.

In short, I took away many of the methods I had used to validate my self-worth. Guess what? It worked! I no longer got the looks from men that I had been used to. For the most part, it seemed as if I was invisible to them except for the few who reacted to my new look with revulsion. In some ways those years were like a twilight zone. I no longer got my validation from the outside world, yet my connection to myself was so tenuous, there were times I actually questioned my existence. *Who was I?*

During this time I had no relationships with men because I didn't want to continue in the patterns I had learned to express my sexuality. In fact, looking back, I see that—again, as some nuns do—I decided sexuality was something I needed to transcend if I was ever going to find my true self. Oddly enough, though, this perpetuated the same struggle as before, but now for different reasons. This period of great change did prove to be valuable—eventually I learned to be more self-connected—but it was in no way a magical cure.

SHARING OUR FANTASIES

Garry's looking at porn had stimulated me to relive the inner struggle that had started in my childhood. And in turn, when I had expressed my feelings about his use of porn, he had relived his painful sexual history. It took time to sort through the confusion and reach the point where we understood where these feelings were coming from. Each day, we chose to keep working at it, believing that it presented an opportunity to find our way through the maze of conditioning that had created so much suffering for both of us over the years. We wanted to trust that our relationship could help heal our pasts and that we could support each other's healing by shining the light on our old pain.

Here is what we came up with: The parts of ourselves that felt desire and that we had labeled bad in the past wanted freedom of expression. The parts of ourselves we had labeled as good were the parts that wanted to conform and to suppress desire; this was how we could be valued and loved by others who labeled such behaviors as good. Once we opened our hearts to both sides of ourselves, it was easier to invite both desire and the wish to control it into our lives—without judgment and without making either side wrong. We ended up having a whole lot of fun!

To support the integration of these parts of ourselves, we decided to share and act out our sexual fantasies with each other. We agreed we wouldn't shame, blame, or judge, and that we'd stop when either one of us became uncomfortable.

GARRY: *Even though I had looked at porn and read sex stories almost every day until recently, I didn't have what I would call freedom around sex. Somehow I was caught in a cycle that had me reinforcing my judgments about myself; I knew that looking at porn wasn't the answer. Now, what I was looking for was a way to see my fantasies in a different light or on another level. My hope was that as Victoria and I brought these parts of ourselves out into an environment where they were held with love and care, they might tell us something about ourselves that we couldn't see before.*

So we started revealing our fantasies to each other. It was both exciting and terrifying! This experiment was more challenging for me because I labored against a much stronger inhibition about expressing fantasies; maybe Garry's experience with porn had helped lessen some of his restraints. But he had some difficulty expressing his fantasies as well. Both of us brought to this journey conditioning that judged sexual fantasies as bad, especially the more taboo aspects.

Sometimes we put a lot of time and effort into crafting our fantasies, telling each other what they were about from start to finish, detailing the other's role and specifying what to say. Other times it was more off the cuff, and we gave each other the gist of the story and ad-libbed from there.

Once we got the hang of it, we enjoyed giving voice and expression to our fantasies. We found that our play helped us to connect with one another, and also that it was an adventurous, creative learning experience. I noticed physical effects as well, feeling more connected to my body. I moved differently, with more movement in my hips, and I wasn't as *locked up* in my pelvic area. I also realized I wasn't as squeamish about sex talk and sex scenes: prior to all these fun and games, if a movie went into a sex scene, I had found myself tensing and holding my breath until it was over. As we continued expressing our fantasies, I found I could fall into those scenes and not push them away.

GARRY: *I seemed to have more energy, and it was fanning out into other areas like work and an interest in getting out more. I saw that I had reduced the energy of desire by equating it with only sex, but once I was able to free it up some, I realized it was actually the spark of all life. I thought about what urged me to do anything in life and saw that it was created out of this amazing energy of desire.*

I had a belief that if I had particular fantasies that I labeled as wrong, I had to keep them suppressed for fear I might act on them. But once I started giving them breathing room, my fear of acting them out in real life lessened. I no longer doubted myself in the way I had before. My confidence and trust in myself grew, and I became very clear on the distinctions between fantasy and reality. This was a huge relief to me.

One day after we finished having sex, I began to cry.

"What is it?" Garry asked while he held me.

"I'm not sure," I sniffled. "I think I'm sad because playing these roles didn't work for me today, and I didn't pay attention to that voice that didn't want to play."

"Is it that you weren't as connected to yourself and

what your needs were as you would have liked?" Garry asked.

"Yes," I replied. "And doing something I wasn't really into just didn't feel right—like I wasn't in alignment with my own authenticity and integrity." I thought for a moment longer and then added, "I notice that lately I've been feeling worried that when we do this we're missing out on really seeing one another. I guess maybe I want to be sure that you can make love to me, not some image of what you want me to be, and that I can be with you and not just a fantasy in my head." I paused again. "Do you know what I mean?"

"I think so. You want to be sure that when we're making love I'm seeing who you are and not just my projection of a fantasy. Is that it?"

"Yes, that's it ... I'm curious. What happens for you when I say all that?"

It was Garry's turn to be quiet for a moment. "I can relate to what you're saying, but I don't think that I'm ever not making love to you when we're role-playing. It's the chemistry of you and me together, and the love and trust we share with one another, that I connect with every time we play like this."

"I like what you're saying, and I believe that's true for me too, so maybe part of my being upset is that I'm looking for more balance." I reflected on this as we lay together quietly. "I guess maybe I want to know that we can have sex without having to role-play, that we can be just us and have that be okay too. It's funny, because even though I'm in a fantasy the same as you when we have sex, I want to blame you for the pain I'm having right now. When I really think about it, I realize I'm projecting onto you what I want for myself—to be more present to myself and to you during our lovemaking."

It seemed that our role-playing, which had once been so liberating, was now too confining. It took a while before we were able to take this understanding to the next level. We continued to share our fantasies, and they began to feel a bit hit or miss—sometimes satisfying, sometimes not—and sometimes we didn't do fantasies at all. We couldn't figure out why on some days one particular fantasy worked for us and on other days it didn't.

NEEDS IN FANTASIES

One day, during a drowsy conversation after sex, we noted that fantasies had a quality very similar to dreams. A common form of dream analysis holds that in any given dream we ourselves are all the characters within that dream, with each representing a different aspect of self. We realized that our fantasies were similar in that the roles we played represented different parts of ourselves that wanted expression.

Further, we saw that not only did they want expression, but our fantasies were able to show us what was important to us in our lives—in other words, what needs we were trying to meet. This was why some fantasies had a lot of life for us while others fell flat: the ones that had a lot of life met more important needs than did others. For example, if it's important to me to experience a sense of power or have more control in my life, I might be attracted to a more aggressive or dominating fantasy. Being tied up isn't going to do it for me because it doesn't serve that need. And it works the other way too;

if I already control much of my life and I want to experience letting go, then being tied up may feel right to me.

We were so excited to make this discovery; it seemed
like the next step we had been looking for! Bringing our
fantasies out into the open had helped free us from our
shame, but this new idea just might take our awareness
to a whole other level, helping us understand the driving force behind them. We started making connections
right away. Garry's predominant themes had to do with
innocence and power. His favorite fantasy scenario involved an innocent, inexperienced young maiden who
was his for the taking.

GARRY: *In my fantasy the young woman trusts me
completely. She desires to please me and is there
for me 100 percent. I don't have to give anything
back, just receive. And she has what I call a look of
innocence, something open. I can see trust in that
look—whereas, so I tell myself, older women are
more protective and guarded— they've lost the innocent naiveté.*

*In the past I felt a lot of shame because I believed
that there was something wrong with me for fantasizing about young women. But when I could look
at it from the perspective that it told me something
important about myself, I started to see it in a whole
new light.*

*I saw that I was seeking my own innocence.
Early on in my life I learned to cover up my own
authenticity, and I became hardened to life. I had a
lot of shame about my body and my desires, and I
learned to hide them. What I looked for in pictures
and in fantasies was something that reminded me*

of what I had lost: openness and trust. I wanted
something that reminded me of the lovability and
vulnerability in myself. When my fantasy partners
did whatever I wanted, it gave me a sense of power
that I just didn't seem to have in my everyday life.

Seeing my fantasies in this way was life-chang-
ing for me. Before, I had been caught in thinking
that there was something outside myself that I
needed in order to be whole or complete—now I
could see that it was an inside job. I felt exuberant
as I sensed the kind of power in my world I had been
wanting. It was no longer outside and unattainable;
it had been a part of me all along, but I just couldn't
see it.

I was excited that Garry was claiming his life in this way, and eager to see what my fantasies could tell me. I now saw them as precious storybooks that could reveal hidden treasures buried in my psyche.

What was most interesting about my fantasies was that I was never in them! They were always about imaginary figures, and it was as though I cast them for roles in my own private movies. As I thought about the part of me that believed sex wasn't safe, it made sense to me that I would create stand-ins for myself who could experience what was ultimately too scary for me. My invisibility created a shield. As for the scripts themselves, I was fond of scenes where rough pirate types lurked like spiders in corners and lured poor innocent girls into their webs. These girls didn't give themselves over willingly, but they were secretly excited and they liked what was happening.

The woman in each fantasy was like a character in a

dream. Even though she didn't look like me, she still represented a part of me. I realized this fantasy was playing out my inability to figure out how to be a *good* girl and still have sex, so I developed a strategy in my fantasies that allowed me to keep my value intact and enjoy sex at the same time by having it taken from me. Brilliant! Then I wondered about the man in my fantasy—was he part of me as well? Yes, I thought so. He was pure lust that didn't need to hold back in any way or keep himself in check; he could do as he pleased. God, how I had longed for this kind of freedom with my own sexuality, just to be free to do as *I* pleased. He was a reminder of how I wanted to take the constraints off my own sexuality.

Seeing our fantasies in this way was intriguing to me, and it inspired even more thoughts. I wondered what would happen if I could connect to these needs in my everyday life more consciously. Would it shift my desire to play them out in my fantasies? I wanted to know, so I consciously chose to connect with my own inner experience of freedom and value, not knowing where it would take me.

More Exploration

Garry and I hadn't told ourselves that we *had* to have sex "x" times per month in order to be happy, but we did settle into a routine of having it once or twice a week on average. He initiated it most of the time—and when he stopped initiating, I started freaking out a bit. I wondered, *Does he still love me? Is he losing his attraction for me?! Oh no, I've heard that marriage can do this to people!*

After a couple of weeks of no sex, I told him I missed it and asked if anything was going on. At first he was only able to articulate that he just didn't feel like it, but he assured me that all was well with him otherwise. I believed him when he said all was well because in some ways we were closer than ever, so we continued to snuggle for long periods of time, and we talked freely about lots of different things. I didn't experience any static between us. And yet, time passed ... and still no sex.

When we explored some different possibilities of what might be going on for him, Garry told me he still wasn't sure, but he now wondered if maybe something might be wrong, like an undetected illness. Before I could talk about how scared that thought made me, he told me he was wondering about another possibility—that he had been increasingly uncomfortable with the way we were having sex. He said he might be experiencing the same thing I had earlier: maybe the role-playing wasn't working for him anymore either. I breathed a sigh of relief. Then I wondered what might be precipitating this change in us. Was it possible that we no longer needed the fantasies as much because we had made our needs more conscious? I didn't know, but I was curious to see where this was going to go.

GARRY: *I'm not sure what was happening to me because it was more about what was not happening to me. It seemed like one day I just lost my desire for sex. It's not that I didn't want to have it with Victoria or that I wanted to go back to looking at porn and masturbating; instead it was nothing, zip, nada, no sexual interest at all!*

I did have an aversion to anything that created

distance between myself and a direct experience of
what I was doing, so when Victoria and I talked or
just held one another, that was even more wonder-
ful than it had been before because I was more pres-
ent. And when it came to not desiring sex, I wasn't
too worried because I wasn't pulling away from our
relationship. In fact, I was more fully in it.

One day Garry and I were on a walk, talking about where he was in his process. I asked him if he thought that this pause in our sex life could be a recalibration of his sexual energies, that maybe he had been so used to being stimulated by so many images in pornography that this might be his body's way of aligning itself with where he was now.

GARRY: *Something about that recalibration theory rang*
true for me. It was as if the old way just wasn't
working for me anymore and I needed the time and
space to figure out what I did want. In some ways
it was like being in the wilderness without a map. I
had been letting go of so many ways I related to my-
self and others sexually, but hadn't any ideas about
how I would relate. Now what? It came down to
trusting that I would figure it out as time went by.
At times I sensed Victoria's urgency to talk about
what was going on, but for the most part she seemed
willing to ride it out with me.

Time went by, a couple of weeks turned into a month, and then a month turned into a month and a half … still nothing. I wanted to respect the unfolding and timing of Garry's process without putting any pressure on him, so

I instead turned my attentions to what was going on for me. Now that we weren't having sex, it was like a structure was gone from our lives. It was somewhat scary, but it also gave us an opportunity to do things differently.

My first inclination was to attach my own sense of worth to his not wanting to have sex: if he didn't want to have sex (with me) then I wasn't worth having sex with. I decided to see if instead I could hold my own value and sense of self separate from Garry's, disconnect it entirely from his desire for sex. After all, my fantasies pointed me to the need to connect with my own value. Almost immediately, my fears about his loss of desire decreased. I also noticed that I had been fashioning my life around his desires since we'd begun our relationship. In waiting for him to initiate sex, I was, again, allowing his desire to dictate my sexual worthiness. But what about my own desires? Could I let the guy in my fantasies come out and play? And if so, what would that look like?

Not long after that day, I got some answers to my questions. Instead of being the good girl and waiting for him to dictate whether or not we had sex, I let my own sexual energies direct me. Being in touch with them, I spontaneously reached out for Garry to make love. For some reason it just seemed right, and it was. Garry responded eagerly. We didn't play roles. Garry was Garry and I was me, and we were fully present with each other. And it was beautiful, simple, and profound.

Just for the record, our fantasy life didn't go away; on the contrary, it's richer than ever. What's different is that we're no longer run by shame and we're in touch with the life behind our fantasies that wants expression. Being in touch with that life gives us greater connection to ourselves and each other, taking lovemaking to a much more satisfying level for both of us.

chapter 12:
The End of the Perfect Ending ...
or a New Beginning?

As we worked through the chapters of this book, we began to wonder how we would end it. Would the last chapter be a fairy-tale ending with all our problems resolved and the two of us living happily ever after? Then something happened that challenged us both to the core. It made us question everything we had written so far. Had we deluded ourselves? Was our message really worthy of sending out into the world? Could we pretend that what we are about to relate here in this final chapter hadn't really happened? Ultimately, we found the strength and connection to rise above our doubts and fears.

We realized that we could not face you, our readers, with honesty and integrity if we did not include this chapter. Furthermore, we believe that this experience demonstrates the value of all that we have learned. We hope sharing this story helps you see that embarking on a journey such as ours doesn't end life's challenges; it's gaining the tools to deal with those challenges that is so valuable. So, it is with this knowledge in our minds and in our hearts that we once again share our truth.

DISCONNECTION

It was in the fall of last year. I had gone to bed early after watching a movie on slavery, upset at how Africans had been used as commodities, not seen as human beings. I lay there for a while, trying to get the horrific images I had seen out of my head. I couldn't shake them, and I finally decided that closing down, not talking about what was going on for me, was an old coping mechanism that I just didn't want to use anymore. I walked into the living room to find Garry so I could talk through my angst—and a wave of fear washed through me as I sensed him tensing at the computer.

He got up quickly and sat beside me on the couch. I noted but ignored my fear of what he might have been doing, thinking that my reaction might be coming from the sensitive emotional place I was in. Instead, I poured out my sorrow about slavery. I agonized aloud about the way it had been, and still can be, for people of color in this country, and I told him how I longed to live in a world that honored everyone's humanity. As I talked, my sorrow eased and I felt better, though the cruel images I had seen still haunted me. I realized anew how important it was to me that everyone be treated with respect and care, and I was happy I had chosen to express my feelings instead of keeping them bottled up. At last I was ready for bed, and I stood up to leave the room.

Garry got up quickly, went to the computer, and asked me if I wanted him to shut it down. Again a wave of fear washed over me. He seemed anxious to me, a little too eager. I didn't meet his eyes as I told him I'd do it after I checked my e-mail. Garry switched the computer over to my user side and left to brush his teeth. I waited a moment, struggling with myself: I wanted to see what he'd been doing, but I was afraid of what it could mean if I found porn.

Finally, I just had to look. Maybe it was my emotional turmoil from the movie, maybe it was instinct. Whatever was at work, I clicked back to his user screen. My heart dropped as pages and pages of pictures of nude young women popped up, and my wave of fear turned into a tsunami. What was going on? How long had he been concealing this from me? After all we'd been through, after his decision to stop and his intention to talk to me if it came up again, how could he hide it from me? Over and over, he had told me how important it was for him to be honest about this very thing! Who *was* this guy? Had everything been a lie?

Shaking, I made my way to the bathroom and stood there watching him brush his teeth, wondering just who I was looking at. Was he still the guy I thought I knew, or was he so buried in his desire to please that I only saw the Garry he wanted me to see? Finally I said, "How long have you been looking at porn and not telling me?" He turned to me with deer-in-the-headlights eyes and the toothbrush still in his mouth. I didn't wait for him to answer, but simply turned and went back to the living room.

He joined me there and we just sat for a while, neither of us saying a word. My mind was racing, but shock had rendered me speechless. Finally I was able to ask again, "How long have you been looking at porn and not telling me?"

He didn't look at me. "About a month now."

I took that in. For a month we had been living with

a lie between us. My anger and confusion rose as my needs for honesty, trust, and authenticity screamed for attention.

"Why?"

"Why what?"

I just waited.

He finally looked at me. "I'm not sure. I think it might have something to do with working so much lately and talking about buying a house. I have that old feeling of a huge weight of responsibility on my shoulders. Every time we crunch the numbers to see if we can afford it, I think I'm going to be working for the rest of my life, and I get pissed off. Porn seems to help me feel better somehow."

Something in his words rang true, which helped ease my anger and hurt a little. We *had* been stressed with the thought of buying a house, and I was aware of his propensity to take on responsibility and shut down in the face of it. It sounded as if, with the added stress in his life, he was reverting back to old coping strategies.

Then he said something that caught me up short, "Also ... it seems like you've been distant lately."

Confusion and anger flooded back through me, and my old belief that I have to do all kinds of things to make people love me was at full throttle. I heard his words as an accusation: if I hadn't been distant, this wouldn't have happened. In other words, if I wasn't demonstrative enough, or considerate enough about his needs, then I would lose him to porn. Anger won over confusion, and the door to my heart that had opened a crack slammed shut with a bang.

"So where am I in all of this, Garry?" I hissed. "Did you ever stop to think about how this was going to impact me and our relationship? Through all of our struggles with porn, I cherished your desire to be open and honest. That's all that made this whole situation tolerable—I trusted that you would tell me what was going on for you. Why would you not tell me after you said you would, and all the times I've told you how much I value that? I just don't get it! I could partially understand if I had given you an ultimatum, but we chose a different route, one based on being real. If we don't have that ... I'm afraid of what it might mean."

My anger was subsiding and morphing into sadness. I began to cry in despair. I was terrified that Garry's desire for porn was bigger than us. We sat there for a long while until we both realized we were tired and didn't have the capacity to deal with something so huge. It also seemed that Garry didn't have many answers for me that night, so we went to bed—but I slept in the spare room.

THE TURNING POINT

GARRY: *I couldn't sleep much that night. I was very worried about what this might do to our relationship. This fear lit a fire under me and motivated me to figure out what the heck was going on. No more telling myself it was okay to be hiding out.*

I lay there retracing my steps back into porn. Even though my desire to look at it had diminished, and for a while it had seemed easy to not look at it, the urge had never gone completely. It hovered in the background, and I was often tempted by an ad or a revealing photo on the internet. About a month earlier I had been searching online for websites we might want to feature this book on. Plugging in the word pornography brought up lots of sites I had to sift through and lots of temptations I tried to resist. I eventually found myself thinking, "Nudes are not really porn. I'll just check this one out. She'll never know." One thing led to another and pretty soon I was back to looking at porn and hiding that fact.

But why did I hide it when I'd worked so hard at being honest with Victoria? When I had told her I'd stopped looking at porn, she was so happy. I could tell that she trusted me more and was giving more of herself to me in ways that I really liked. There was a wonderful ease between us that hadn't been there since porn had become an issue. I didn't want that to go away. I knew how much she had struggled when I looked at porn, and I was afraid that if she knew I had gone back to it she would finally throw in the towel and leave.

There was also this book. After all the work we'd put into it, I wanted the book to end on a positive note. Didn't we have to have a nice Hollywood ending where we rode off into the sunset, each happy and giving others hope? If I was honest with her about going back to looking at porn, wouldn't that make everything we had done moot? Or worse, a sham?

Still, something else lingered, but I couldn't quite get at it. I was sure it had to do with needs—if I'd learned anything in our struggles, it was that I was trying to meet needs and if I could just see them it would help me put the pieces together. It wasn't just the ever-present enticements online. There were other things going on as well.

A few months back I had gotten a promotion at work that meant taking on a lot of responsibility as the head of a team with many others involved. I had shied away from that kind of position in the past. My usual MO had been to focus on my own part of a project and leave the rest up to others. In this new position I was responsible for coordinating other people's work, and I feared the stress. To top it off, we'd been thinking of buying a home, and that was turning out to feel like another huge burden.

Then there was Victoria herself. She really had seemed distant lately, not as interested in me or in us. It seemed like she'd been preoccupied, and that scared me.

Somewhere in the middle of the night I took a deep breath and knew that it was up to me. It was make or break time. I was an adult, and taking on adult responsibilities at work—and at home—was no longer something I wanted to avoid. I would develop the skills it took to deal with them.

And Victoria? I loved her more than I had ever thought possible. If she'd been distant, I needed to ask her about it, to find out why. I wanted to take positive action instead of reverting to my old coping mechanisms.

I closed my eyes and hoped we could get through this.

I couldn't sleep much that night either. Alone, without my beloved, I tossed and turned, feeling both hurt and despair. Doubts about our relationship ran through my head. I thought about all that we had talked about and everything we had learned, and I wanted to chuck it all—including the book we had written—thinking that it was just a bunch of hooey. Then I realized there was something here worth holding on to. Thinking back over the profound, life-changing journey we had made together, I decided that I wasn't ready to give up yet. Not on Garry, not on our relationship. Yes, I was angry. And yes, I was hurting. But I also had to believe that his heart was in the right place and that he wasn't consciously trying to hurt me.

My mind kept coming back to our needs, his and mine. I tried to sink into and connect with the ones that were important to me that hadn't been met by his actions. Trust and honesty were among them, but I think what I wanted most was to know that he was able to consider my needs in any given moment. I also wondered what needs could possibly have been so strong for him that he would hide them from me. Wearily, I rolled over and looked at the clock one last time. Four a.m. I closed my eyes and fell asleep at last.

Reconnecting

I awoke the next morning from the refuge of sleep, and then I remembered the night before: my stomach pitched. I rolled over and pulled the pillow over my head. One part of me didn't want to face the day, but I also wanted to find a way to reconnect with Garry. Extricating myself from the pillow, I looked up to find him already standing at the door. "Wanna talk?" he asked. He looked tired and sad.

I said yes. When I got up and made it over to the mirror, I could see that I looked pretty rough myself.

An hour later we sat down across from one another and Garry began to speak. "First, I want to apologize for breaking my promise to you. I was caught in a struggle, and I resorted to hiding a part of myself as I often have in the past. I want to stop doing that.

"I didn't sleep much last night, but now I think I have a better handle on what's been going on for me. I think one part of what happened was that I was up against some old stuff that I've always tried to avoid. One of the ways I've dealt with stress in the past has been to use porn to distract myself. I think some of these patterns are so unconscious that I couldn't even see them in order to deal with them."

"Like what?" I asked, eager to hear some explanation.

"I'm not sure why it's so strong," Garry said, "but it seems that every time I think I'm responsible for things, I get really anxious. With this new position at work, plus the thought of buying a house, I think I feared I was getting trapped."

I knew this about him and instantly linked it back to his childhood, where, as the eldest brother, he was supposed to be the *man* of the house—and resented it.

"So is it freedom that's so important to you?"

"Yes. And something else that I'm not sure how to express ... I want to know that I don't have to give up myself for others. At work, I fear I'll end up working long hours and taking on tasks that I don't want to do, and with buying a home I'm afraid I'll have to work the rest of my life to pay it off. I want to be free to do things I really enjoy instead of working all the time."

I felt my anger rising again. "Garry, what does porn have to do with any of that? Looking at porn isn't going to help you set boundaries at work, nor is it going to help you not buy a home if that's what you want."

"I know that. And if I had been better able to identify what was going on for me, I think I would have been able to see it. But porn has often been the strategy I employ to get relief from this fear of responsibility. For some reason it's wrapped up with freedom from something I don't quite see yet. But I do know that if I can't see what's going on for me when I'm anxious or stressed, it's all too easy to go right back to it."

We stared at each other for awhile. I was starting to understand, but I still felt anger that was calling for my attention. "It helps me to see that," I told him, "but I have to say that right now I am still really pissed at you. I know that sometimes we can't always see things clearly right away, but even so, where am I in all of this, Garry? I'm not hearing anything about your being concerned how this will impact me and us! Did you stop to consider what my needs might be?"

Garry didn't answer right away, then quietly said, "I don't know. I told myself that it wouldn't hurt you because you were never going to know. I do know I was afraid to tell you because I didn't want to disappoint you."

I couldn't believe it—how could he think finding out without being told was somehow better?

"*This* disappoints me Garry. I don't want perfection, I want to know you and what's going on for you. After all we've been through I guess I'm shocked that you still don't get that. I want to know that you're able to hold my needs as important in any given situation. I get it—your need for freedom was raising its head, and I want you to have what you need. But I also want you to be able to look over here and see how what you do might impact me!"

"I truly want that too, Victoria, because I love you and your needs are important to me. I think that, in my confusion about how to deal with this responsibility issue, I couldn't keep a clear perspective of your needs as well as my own. I fell back into distracting myself with porn and told myself that concealing it was enough. But the truth is, I felt fear and shame about it, and that tells me my actions weren't meeting my needs for integrity or honesty."

My fury began to dissipate, and I could feel the connection between us strengthen. And I couldn't believe how easily that had happened. It seemed like one moment I was in full-blown rage and ready to do God knows what, and in the next I was settled and back to loving this guy. Oddly enough, what struck me most in that moment was that I no longer got lost so easily in judgments about whether his looking at porn was right or wrong; instead, I could hear what the message behind it was. Had we not worked so hard to grasp the understanding of needs, I would have missed the beauty behind his actions, as well as the beauty in my pain. Getting down to our needs was once again leading us back to connection with ourselves and each other.

I was reveling in this awareness when Garry said, "There's more. Are you ready to hear what else I've been thinking about?"

"Sure," I said. I was already pleased that we had

achieved such understanding, and surprised that there was more to come. A wave of gratitude washed over me as I realized how much I loved Garry's ability to eventually see what was going on and share that with me.

"I've been experiencing you as being somewhat distant lately, not as demonstrative as you usually are, and I got scared. Last night I realized that for much of my life I've had a belief that I need women in order to be happy—consequently I've given women the power to control my life and my happiness. I'm terrified when I think about how much I need you. Terrified! It's so scary that I haven't allowed myself to see it clearly until now. I think it's one of the reasons I couldn't talk to you about it. To do that, I would have had to admit to myself how extremely vulnerable I feel, and I don't think I was ready.

"When I feel this terror, it's easy to go to porn. It's been the one place where the fear dissipates, because I don't have to be afraid of those women. I interpreted your distance in my own way, as the threat that you weren't happy, so I was scared to talk to you about it. And then I went to my safe haven, the one place I have control of women in my life. Now that I can see this, and I have admitted it to myself, I hope it won't be so difficult for me to name it next time and give myself the option to do something different—like telling you that I feel lonely."

I had the sense that Garry was getting to some core value in himself, and I was excited by it. And I relaxed even more when I heard him make those connections. I believe that when we gain awareness about what is truly motivating our actions, we're less likely to wreak havoc in our world. I felt myself opening to him once again.

"I love what you just shared, Garry, because I now have some hope that we can start looking at what's really going on instead of focusing on your strategy to avoid it. I don't need to have your desire to look at porn all wrapped up and put away like you don't have it anymore. I just want to know that you're being honest with me about where you are with it. I want to know that you're able to consider my needs as well."

"Yeah," Garry said, "I think I really understand that now. I've kept parts of myself hidden from others for so many years of my life that it's easy to fall back on that strategy when I'm stressed. I think it's really taking some time—longer than I thought it would—to finally get that I don't have to do that anymore. I've been focused on the question of whether or not I look at porn, but even more important is the question of who I want to be in this relationship with you."

We held each other in silence for a while, back to our solid connection with one another. I thought about Garry's concern that I had been distant. "I know what you mean about me being distant," I said. "Maybe I was sensing stresses brewing below the surface but I wasn't aware enough to address it. It's kind of funny in a sad way, because I was doing the same thing you were, using my old strategy of going off into my own world instead of asking you about it. It's odd that we were both reinforcing our disconnection with each other by not discussing it. As I become more conscious of this pattern I would like to be able to check in with you instead of making assumptions."

"Yes, I want to do more of that as well."

We sat quietly for a little while longer, and then Garry said with wonder, "Are you aware of how easy it was for us to reconnect, compared to the prolonged anger and pain we would have experienced in the past? It almost makes me question whether we're avoiding something. But it just doesn't feel like we are."

"Yes!" I exclaimed. "I was thinking about that before. It's great to see how much easier it is for us to connect with what's beneath our actions and go directly to the essence of what's really going on instead of getting stuck fighting about who's right. Now that we know how to get at the needs beneath our actions, we have a lot more choice about how to resolve any situation. Honestly, I'm not sure I would have been able to deal with this one if we hadn't learned all that we have in the last couple of years."

"I know what you mean. Sometimes it seems like it's too good to be true, but now I can't imagine going back to the way things used to be."

That night when we were back together in the same bed, I actually felt grateful for what we'd been through the night before. We had learned something about connecting with and trusting each other, even when our ability to do so was most challenged.

INTERCONNECTEDNESS

There was more to come from this event. I could sense that Garry was working on something at his core, and it turned out to generate some pretty powerful insights. The following week he seemed to be living more internally than he had been recently, as if he had withdrawn into himself to work something out. At first I worried that he was hiding out, but when I asked him about it, he said that he was more conscious than he had ever been and that he could tell he was close to understanding something big about himself.

GARRY: *There was something about this last time looking at porn and having Victoria discover it that helped me to see something about myself more clearly. It had been there all along, but for whatever reasons I couldn't put it all together until then.*

A while back, Victoria had told me about a talk Robert Gonzales gave on dependence, independence, and interdependence. I heard what she was saying at the time, but it didn't really ring any bells for me. Now it was making sense, and I could see how it applied to longtime patterns in my life.

Dependence, as I understand it, is a way to meet one's own needs by focusing on the needs of others. So in my case, when I'm in relationship, I try to figure out my partner's needs and fulfill them so she will love me. Unfortunately, this has me so focused on the other person that I forget to tend to my own needs. Even though I was changing and was much truer to myself after a few years of exploration with Victoria, I still had a tendency to try to figure out what she wanted so she would love me. After I stopped looking at porn, I could see that she loved being with a guy who didn't look at porn, and I still wanted her to love me, so I hid the part of me who still wanted to look.

Then, because dependence didn't meet my need for freedom, I started getting resentful and antsy, and I swung over into independence. Independence is when I focus solely on meeting my own needs and I don't want to consider the other person's. As if in reaction to leaving myself out of the equation previously, I make myself the only person in the equation. This side of things had me thinking things like, "I don't care whether she likes porn or not, I'm going to do what I please." This side wanted the freedom to be who I am without having to consider others.

These two opposing sides seemed to conflict in my life. One wanted intimacy and to be loved while the other resented the demands that seemed to come with those things, and I wanted the freedom to be myself. I didn't know how to get the love I wanted and be myself at the same time. This was a conundrum.

In the world of porn, that conflict simply didn't exist; it was one of the main reasons I found it so alluring. I could meet some needs for intimacy with it because it gave me some kind of interaction with women, but I didn't lose my connection with myself, and I still had my freedom. Yes, it was fantasy, but it often seemed better than struggling with a real relationship. It was a gigantic rest stop from a seemingly never-ending pendulum swinging back and forth from dependence to independence.

I realized that Victoria had been asking me for interdependence again and again in this relationship. She wanted me to be able to hold on to my needs and be myself, even if she didn't always agree with what I did, and to be able to consider her needs at the same time. I hadn't really understood that until now. This relationship wasn't about only my

needs or only her needs or doing things we thought
were necessary to keep the relationship together. It
was about having both our needs acknowledged and
valued, and reflected in our actions.

   Now I'm trusting more and more that I can have
intimacy and freedom at the same time.

Holy smokes! When Garry shared this discovery with me, I almost couldn't believe my ears! I was amazed that he had been able to make those connections, and his insights had me loving him more than ever—not to mention helping me see more clearly the same pattern in my own life. I, too, had been swinging back and forth from dependence to independence for as long as I could remember. I would focus on another's needs, trying to get the love I wanted, until I could no longer deny myself my own needs—or consider the needs of my partner at all. Often at this point, I left the relationship: it was the only thing I could think to do. Then, once on my own and taking care of myself again, my need for love and intimacy would emerge and, voilà, I'd jump into another relationship. I knew that I was still doing this dependence-independence dance with Garry to some degree, but now I had more hope that I would be able to identify and name this pattern for myself—and live more in interdependence.

A New Beginning

And so we move forward once again.

Yes, we are once more headed into uncharted territory, and I love being in a relationship that has this much life in it. I'm excited about our future together, about living in an interdependent relationship and what that will mean. I believe we're stepping into a new way of loving, one I have never experienced before, one that holds love and freedom at the same time. One in which we can hold on to what is important to each of us, and each other, at the same time. I am excited and honored to be walking this path with the man I love so much.

I did want a perfect ending for this book. I wanted an ending that gave hope to everyone who was struggling with the issue of pornography, something that they could use to deal with it once and for all. I wanted a "happily ever after"—for myself and for you.

But this is not a movie, and we can't wrap it up with a nice, neat bow. We can give you our honesty and our truth and our hope that the future only gets better as our insights build and grow.

This path continues to help us find hope and to value each other more. We relish the opportunity each moment brings us to see ourselves and each other in our essence. We believe that is what the great adventure of relationship is all about. Our fondest hope is that this book we have created supports you in finding your way to your own path.

Gilda Radner once said, "I wanted a perfect ending. Now I've learned, the hard way, that some poems don't rhyme, and some stories don't have a clear beginning, middle, and end. Life is about not knowing, having to change, taking the moment and making the best of it without knowing what's going to happen next."

So in the spirit of Gilda, Garry and I have let go of the perfect ending and are sailing off into the unknown once again—into our very own kind of "happily ever after," filled with the knowledge that we are ever growing, ever loving, and ever hopeful.

Appendix:
Feelings and Needs

The following lists of feelings and needs—feelings and needs "inventories"—were taken directly from the Center for Nonviolent Communication website and are available to everyone. Please see contact information on the last page.

FEELINGS INVENTORY

The following are words we use when we want to express a combination of emotional states and physical sensations. This list is neither exhaustive nor definitive. It is meant as a starting place to support anyone who wishes to engage in a process of deepening self-discovery and to facilitate greater understanding and connection between people.

There are two parts to this list: feelings you may have when your needs are being met and feelings you may have when your needs are not being met.

Feelings when your needs are satisfied

AFFECTIONATE
compassionate
friendly
loving
open hearted
sympathetic
tender
warm

CONFIDENT
empowered
open
proud
safe
secure

ENGAGED
absorbed
alert
curious
engrossed
enchanted
entranced
fascinated
interested
intrigued
involved
spellbound
stimulated

EXCITED
amazed
animated
ardent
aroused
astonished
dazzled
eager
energetic
enthusiastic
giddy
invigorated
lively
passionate
surprised
vibrant

EXHILARATED
blissful
ecstatic
elated
enthralled
exuberant
radiant
rapturous
thrilled

GRATEFUL
appreciative
moved
thankful
touched

HOPEFUL
expectant
encouraged
optimistic
trusting

INSPIRED
amazed
awed
wonder

JOYFUL
amused
delighted
glad
happy
jubilant
pleased
tickled

PEACEFUL
calm
clear headed
comfortable
centered
content
equanimous
fulfilled
mellow
quiet
relaxed
relieved
satisfied
serene
still
tranquil
trusting

REFRESHED
enlivened
rejuvenated
renewed
rested
restored
revived

Feelings when your needs are not satisfied

AFRAID
apprehensive
dread
foreboding
frightened
mistrustful
panicked
petrified
scared
suspicious
terrified
wary
worried

ANGRY
enraged
furious
incensed
indignant
irate
livid
outraged
resentful

ANNOYED
aggravated
dismayed
disgruntled
displeased
exasperated
frustrated

impatient
irritated
irked

AVERSION
animosity
appalled
contempt
disgusted
dislike
hate
horrified
hostile
repulsed

CONFUSED
ambivalent
baffled
bewildered
dazed
hesitant
lost
mystified
perplexed
puzzled
torn

DISCONNECTED

alienated
aloof
apathetic
bored
cold
detached
distant
distracted
indifferent
numb
removed
uninterested
withdrawn

DISQUIET

agitated
alarmed
discombobulated
disconcerted
disturbed
perturbed
rattled
restless
shocked
startled
surprised
troubled

turbulent
turmoil
uncomfortable
uneasy
unnerved
unsettled
upset

EMBARRASSED

ashamed
chagrined
flustered
guilty
mortified
self-conscious

FATIGUE

beat
burnt out
depleted
exhausted
lethargic
listless
sleepy
tired
weary
worn out

PAIN
agony
anguished
bereaved
devastated
grief
heartbroken
hurt
lonely
miserable
regretful
remorseful

SAD
depressed
dejected
despair
despondent
disappointed
discouraged
disheartened
forlorn
gloomy
heavy hearted
hopeless
melancholy
unhappy
wretched

TENSE
anxious
cranky
distressed
distraught
edgy
fidgety
frazzled
irritable
jittery
nervous
overwhelmed
restless
stressed out

VULNERABLE
fragile
guarded
helpless
insecure
leery
reserved
sensitive
shaky

YEARNING
envious
jealous
longing
nostalgic
pining
wistful

Needs Inventory

The following list of needs is neither exhaustive nor definitive. It is meant as a starting place to support anyone who wishes to engage in a process of deepening self-discovery and to facilitate greater understanding and connection between people.

AUTONOMY
choice
freedom
independence
space
spontaneity

CONNECTION
acceptance
affection
appreciation
belonging
cooperation
communication
closeness
community
companionship
compassion
consideration
consistency
empathy

inclusion
intimacy
love
mutuality
nurturing
respect/self-respect
safety
security
stability
support
to know and be known
to see and be seen
to understand and
   be understood
trust
warmth

HONESTY
authenticity
integrity
presence

MEANING

awareness

celebration of life

challenge

clarity

competence

consciousness

contribution

creativity

discovery

efficacy

effectiveness

growth

hope

learning

mourning

participation

purpose

self-expression

stimulation

to matter

understanding

PEACE

beauty

communion

ease

equality

harmony

inspiration

order

PHYSICAL WELL-BEING

air

food

movement/exercise

rest/sleep

sexual expression

safety

shelter

touch

water

PLAY

joy

humor